Theodore Bland Noss

Chapel hymnal

Hymns and songs. Fifth Edition

Theodore Bland Noss

Chapel hymnal
Hymns and songs. Fifth Edition

ISBN/EAN: 9783337266240

Printed in Europe, USA, Canada, Australia, Japan

Cover: Foto ©Thomas Meinert / pixelio.de

More available books at **www.hansebooks.com**

THE CHAPEL HYMNAL.

HYMNS AND SONGS.

.

(FIFTH EDITION.)

Compiled by

THEO. B. NOSS, Ph. D.

[COPYRIGHT, 1899.]

PUBLISHED BY
THE SOUTHWESTERN STATE NORMAL SCHOOL,
CALIFORNIA, PA.

Price 35 cents: $30 per hundred.

PREFACE.

In the compilation of THE CHAPEL HYMNAL an attempt has been made to bring together in a convenient and inexpensive form nearly all of the favorite standard hymns and tunes.

In the selection of "Songs," in the latter part of the book, most of our best patriotic pieces have found a place, together with many other popular songs which the world would not willingly let die. In many institutions it is convenient to have such a collection of the best secular songs included, as an appendix, or second part, of the chapel hymnal. Variety may thus be had in the musical exercises without the expense and inconvenience of an additional book. Teachers of vocal music classes will find in this collection of songs a variety of pleasing and popular airs suitable for class drill.

In the selection of both hymns and songs, particularly of the former, much valuable assistance has been received from several college presidents and from many principals of normal schools and high schools. The compiler of THE CHAPEL HYMNAL gratefully acknowledges his indebtedness to all those who have aided him in the endeavor to collect from all sources the best pieces for this book. He is under obligations, for suggestions and permission to use copyrighted pieces, to several music composers, especially to Dr. H. R. Palmer, whose aid has been most generously given and is here most thankfully acknowledged.

September, 1902.   T. B. N.

The Chapel Hymnal.

No. 1.   Doxology.

THOMAS KEN.   GUILLAUME FRANC.

Praise God, from whom all bless-ings flow; Praise Him, all crea-tures here be - low;

Praise Him a - bove, ye heav'n-ly host; Praise Fa-ther, Son, and Ho - ly Ghost.

No. 2.   Gloria Patri.

Glory be to the Father, and   to the   Son, And to   the Ho - ly Ghost,
As it was in the beginning, is now, and ev - er shall be: World without end. A - men.

No. 3.   Nicæa.   11, 12, 10.

REGINALD HEBER.   Rev. JOHN BACCHUS DY

1. Ho-ly, ho-ly, ho - ly,   Lord   God Al-might - y! Ear - ly in
2. Ho-ly, ho-ly, ho - ly!   All the saints a - dore Thee, Cast-ing dow
3. Ho-ly, ho-ly, ho - ly!   Tho' the dark-ness hide Thee, Tho' the eye
4. Ho-ly, ho-ly, ho - ly,   Lord   God Al-might - y!   All Thy work

morn - ing our song shall rise to Thee;   Ho - ly, ho - ly, ho -
gold-en crowns a-round the glass - y   sea;   Cher - u - bim and sera - p
sin - ful man Thy glo - ry may not see;   On - ly Thou art ho -
praise Thy name, in earth, and sky, and sea;   Ho - ly, ho - ly, ho - l

mer - ci - ful and might-y, God   in Three Per-sons, bless-ed Trin - i - t
fall - ing down be-fore Thee, Which wert, and art, and   ev - er-more shalt b
there is none be - side Thee, Per - fect in pow'r, in   love, and pur - i - t
mer - ci - ful and might-y, God   in Three Per-sons, bless-ed Trin - i - t

No. 4.   Rathbun.   8, 7.

Sir JOHN BOWRING.   ITHAMAR CONK

1. In the cross of   Christ I glo - ry,   Towering o'er the wrecks of tim
2. When the woes of   life o'er-take me,   Hopes de-ceive, and fears an - noy
3. When the sun of   bliss is beam-ing   Light and love up - on my wa
4. Bane and bless-ing, pain and pleas ure,   By the cross are sanc - ti - fied
5. In the cross of   Christ I glo - ry,   Towering o'er the wrecks of tim

Rathbun.

All the light of sa - cred sto - ry / Gath-ers round its head sub-lime.
Nev - er shall the cross for-sake me; / Lo! it glows with peace and joy.
From the cross the ra - diance stream-ing / Adds more lus - ter to the day.
Peace is there that knows no meas-ure, / Joys that thro' all time a - bide.
All the light of sa - cred sto - ry / Gath-ers round its head sub-lime.

No. 5. Eventide. 10.

HENRY F. LYTE. WILLIAM HENRY MONK.

1. A - bide with me! Fast falls the e - ven - tide, The dark-ness
2. Swift to its close ebbs out life's lit - tle day; Earth's joys grow
3. I need Thy pres - ence ev - 'ry pass - ing hour; What but Thy
4. I fear no foe, with Thee at hand to bless; Ills have no
5. Hold Thou Thy cross be - fore my clos - ing eyes; Shine thro' the

deep - ens— Lord, with me a - bide! When oth - er help - ers
dim, its glo - ries pass a - way; Change and de - cay in
grace can foil the tempt-er's pow'r? Who, like Thy - self, my
weight, and tears no bit - ter - ness; Where is death's sting? where,
gloom and point me to the skies; Heav'n's morn-ing breaks, and

fail and com-forts flee, Help of the help-less, O, a - bide with me!
all a-round I see; O Thou. who chang-est not, a - bide with me!
guide and stay can be? Thro, cloud and sunshine, Lord, a - bide with me!
grave, thy vic - to - ry? I tri-umph still, if Thou a - bide with me!
earth's vain shadows flee; In life, in death, O Lord, a - bide with me!

No. 6.   **Uxbridge. L. M.**

ISAAC WATTS.

LOWELL MASON.

1. The heav'ns declare Thy glo - ry, Lord; In ev - 'ry star Thy wis - dom shines;
2. The roll-ing sun, the changing light, And nights and days, Thy pow'r con-fess,
3. Sun, moon, and stars, con-vey Thy praise Round the whole earth, and nev-er stand:
4. Nor shall Thy spread-ing gos-pel rest Till thro' the world Thy truth has run:

But when our eyes be-hold Thy word, We read Thy name in fair - er lines.
But the blest vol-ume Thou hast writ, Re-veals Thy jus-tice and Thy grace.
So when Thy truth be - gan its race, It touched and glanced on ev-'ry land.
Till Christ has all the na-tions blessed That see the light or feel the sun.

No. 7.   **Silver Street. S. M.**

PHILIP DODDRIDGE.

ISAAC SMITH.

1. Grace! 'tis a charm - ing sound, Har - mo - nious to the ear; Heav'n
2. Grace first con-trived a way To save re - bel - lious man; And
3. Grace taught my rov - ing feet To tread the heav'n-ly road; And
4. Grace all the work shall crown Thro' ev - er - last - ing days; It

with the ech - o shall re - sound, And all the earth shall hear.
all the steps that grace dis - play, Which drew the won - drous plan.
new sup-plies each hour I meet, While press - ing on to God.
lays in heav'n the top - most stone, And well de - serves our praise.

No. 8.   Hursley.   L. M.

PETER RITTER.
ARR. BY WILLIAM HENRY MONK.

JOHN KEBLE.

1. Sun of my soul, Thou Sav-ior dear, It is not night if Thou be near;
2. When the soft dews of kind-ly sleep My wear-ied eye- lids gen - tly steep,
3. A-bide with me from morn till eve, For with-out Thee I can - not live;
4. If some poor wand'ring child of Thine Have spurned, to-day, the voice di - vine,
5. Come near and bless us when we wake, Ere thro' the world our way we take;

O, may no earth-born cloud a - rise   To hide Thee from Thy ser-vant's eyes.
Be my last thought, how sweet to rest   For-ev-er on my Sav-ior's breast.
A-bide with me when night is nigh,   For with-out Thee I dare not die.
Now, Lord, the gra-cious work be-gin;   Let him no more lie down in sin.
Till, in the o - cean of Thy love,   We lose our-selves in heav'n a - bove.

No. 9.   Mercy.   7.

LOUIS MOREAU GOTTSCHALK.
ARR BY E. P. PARKER.

GEORGE W. DOANE.

1. Soft - ly now the light of day Fades up - on our sight a - way;
2. Thou, whose all - per-vad-ing eye Naught es-capes, with-out, with - in,
3. Soon from us the light of day Shall for - ev - er pass a - way;

Free from care, from la - bor free,   Lord, we would com-mune with Thee.
Par - don each in-firm - i - ty,   O - pen fault, and se - cret sin.
Then, from sin and sor - row free,   Take us, Lord, to dwell with Thee.

No. 10.   Manoah.   C. M.

JOSEPH ADDISON   FROM F. J. HAYDN.

1. When all Thy mer - cies, O, my God, My ris - ing soul sur - veys,
2. O, how can words with e - qual warmth The grat - i - tude de - clare,
3. Thro' ev - 'ry per - iod of my life Thy good-ness I'll pur - sue;
4. Thro' all e - ter - ni - ty to Thee A grate - ful song I'll raise;

Trans-port - ed with the view, I'm lost In won - der, love and praise.
That glows with - in my rav-ished heart? But Thou canst read it there.
And af - ter death, in dis - tant worlds, The pleas-ing theme re - new.
But O, e - ter - ni - ty's too short To ut - ter all Thy praise.

No. 11.   Evan.   C. M.

FRANCIS ROUS.   WILLIAM HENRY HAVERGAL.

1. The Lord's my Shep herd, I'll not want: He makes me down to lie
2. My soul He doth re - store a - gain; And me to walk doth make
3. Yea, tho' I walk thro' death's dark vale, Yet will I fear no ill;
4. A ta - ble Thou hast fur-nished me In pres ence of my foes;
5. Good-ness and mer - cy all my life Shall sure-ly fol - low me;

In pas-tures green; He lead-eth me The qui - et wa - ters by.
With - in the paths of right-eous-ness, E'en for His own name's sake.
For Thou art with me, and Thy rod And staff me com - fort still.
My head Thou dost with oil a - noint, And my cup o - ver - flows.
And in God's house for ev - er-more My dwell-ing-place shall be.

No. 12.   Tappan.   C. M.

H. KIRKE WHITE.

GEORGE KINGSLEY.

1. The Lord our God is clothed with might, The winds o-bey His will; He speaks, and
2. Re - bel. ye waves, and o'er the land With threat'ning as - pect roar; The Lord up-
3. Ye winds of night, your force combine; Without His high be - hest, Ye shall not,
4. His voice sub-lime is heard a - far; In dis-tant peals it dies; He yokes the
5. Ye sons of earth, in rev'rence bend; Ye na-tions, wait His nod; And bid the

in His heav'nly height He speaks, and in His heav'nly height The rolling sun stands still.
lifts His awful hand, The Lord up-lifts His awful hand, And chains you to the shore.
in the mountain pine, Ye shall not, in the mountain pine, Disturb the spar - row's nest.
whirlwind to His car, He yokes the whirlwind to His car, And sweeps the howling skies.
chor - al song as-cend, And bid the chor-al song as-cend To cel-e - brate our God.

No. 13.   St. Thomas.   S. M.

TIMOTHY DWIGHT.

HANDEL.

1. I love Thy king - dom, Lord, The house of Thine a - bode,
2. I love Thy Church, O God! Her walls be - fore Thee stand,
3. For her my tears shall fall, For her my pray'rs as - cend;
4. Be - yond my high - est joy I prize her heav'n-ly ways,

The Church our blest Re - deem - er saved With His own pre - cious blood.
Dear as the ap - ple of Thine eye, And grav - en on Thy hand.
To her my cares and toils be giv'n, Till toils and cares shall end.
Her sweet com - mun - ion, sol - emn vows, Her hymns of love and praise.

No. 14.   Ariel.   C. P. M.

SAMUEL MEDLEY.   ARR. BY LOWELL MASON.

1. O, could I speak the match-less worth, O, could I sound the glo-ries forth,
2. I'd sing the pre-cious blood He spilt, My ran-som from the dreadful guilt
3. Well, the de-light-ful day will come When my dear Lord will bring me home,

Which in my Sav-ior shine, I'd soar and touch the heav'nly strings, And vie with
Of sin and wrath di-vine; I'd sing His glo-rious right-eous-ness, In which all-
And I shall see His face; Then with my Sav-ior, Broth-er, Friend, A blest e-

Ga-briel while he sings In notes al-most di-vine, In notes al-most di-vine.
per-fect, heav'n-ly dress My soul shall ev-er shine, My soul shall ev-er shine.
ter-ni-ty I'll spend, Tri-umph-ant in His grace, Triumphant in His grace.

No. 15.   Ferguson.   S. M.

PSALM 11.   GEO. KINGSLEY.

1. My trust is in the Lord; How to my soul say ye,
2. Lo, sin-ners bend and bow; On string they fit the dart,
3. What can the right-eous do? What can for them a-vail,
4. The Lord in Zi-on dwells, The Lord's throne is on high:
5. The Lord the right-eous tries; But those that wick-ed be,
6. Fire, brim-stone, snares, fierce storms, On sin-ners He shall rain;
7. Be-cause the right-eous Lord De-lights in right-eous-ness:

Ferguson.

A - way with speed, and like a bird To your high moun-tain flee?
That they un - seen may shoot at those Who up - right are in heart.
If the foun - da - tions be de-stroyed And all they built on fail?
His eyes be - hold the sons of men; Yea, them His eye - lids try.
And him who lov - eth vi - o - lence In soul ab - hor - reth He.
This is the por - tion of their cup, The cup which they shall drain.
And with His gra - cious coun - te - nance The up - right He will bless.

No. 16. Eltham. 7. 61.

HARRIET AUBER. LOWELL MASON.

1. Hast en, Lord, the glo-rious time, When. be-neath Mes-si - ah's sway,
2. Mightiest kings His pow'r shall own; Hea-then tribes His name a - dore;
3. Then shall wars and tu-mults cease; Then be van-ished grief and pain;
4. Bless we, then, our gra-cious Lord; Ev - er praise His glo - rious name;

Ev - 'ry na-tion, ev -'ry clime, Shall the gos-pel call o - bey,
Sa - tan and his host, o'er - thrown, Bound in chains, shall hurt no more,
Righteousness, and joy, and peace, Un-dis-turbed, shall ev - er reign,
All His might-y acts re - cord, All His won-drous love pro - claim,

Ev -'ry na - tion, ev -'ry clime, Shall the gos - pel call o - bey.
Sa - tan and his host o'erthrown, Bound in chains, shall hurt no more.
Right-eous-ness, and joy, and peace, Un-dis-turbed, shall ev - er reign.
All His might - y acts re - cord, All His won-drous love pro - claim.

No. 17. Antioch. C. M.

ISAAC WATTS. ARR. FROM GEO. F. HANDEL.

1. Joy to the world! the Lord is come; Let earth re - ceive her King; Let
2. Joy to the world! the Sav - ior reigns; Let men their songs em-ploy; While
3. No more let sin and sor - row grow, Nor thorns in - fest the ground; He
4. He rules the world with truth and grace, And makes the na-tions prove The

ev - 'ry heart pre-pare Him room, And heav'n and na-ture sing, And
fields and floods, rocks, hills and plains, Re-peat the sound-ing joy, Re-
comes to make His bless-ings flow Far as the curse is found, Far
glo - ries of His right-eous-ness, And won-ders of His love, And

And heav'n, and heav'n and na-ture

heav'n and na - ture sing, And heav'n, and heav'n and na - ture sing.
peat the sound-ing joy, Re - peat, re - peat the sound-ing joy.
as the curse is found, Far as, far as the curse is found.
won-ders of His love, And won-ders, and won - ders of His love.

sing, And heav'n and na-ture sing,

No. 18. Communion. C. M.

ISAAC WATTS. STEPHEN JENKS.

1. A - las! and did my Sav - ior bleed? And did my Sov - 'reign die?
2. Was it for crimes that I have done, He groaned up - on the tree?
3. Well might the sun in dark-ness hide, And shut his glo - ries in,
4. Thus might I hide my blush-ing face While His dear cross ap-pears;
5. But drops of grief can ne'er re - pay The debt of love I owe:

Communion.

Would He de - vote that sa - cred head For such a worm as I?
A - maz - ing pit - y! grace un-known! And love be - yond de - gree!
When Christ, the might-y Mak - er, died, For man the crea - ture's sin.
Dis solye my heart in thank-ful - ness, And melt mine eyes to tears.
Here, Lord, I give my - self a - way—'Tis all that I can do.

No. 19.   Rakem.   L. M.   61.

GEO. W. BETHUNE.
ISAAC BAKER WOODBURY.

1. When time seems short and death is near, And I am pressed by doubt and fear,
2. His name is Je - sus, and He died, For guilt-y sin-ners cru - ci - fied;
3. If grace were bought, I could not buy; If grace were coined, no wealth have I;

And sins, an o - ver-flow-ing tide, As - sail my peace on ev -'ry side,
Con-tent to die that He might win Their ran-som from the death of sin:
By grace a - lone I draw my breath, Held up from ev - er - last-ing death;

This tho't my ref - uge still shall be, I know the Sav - ior died for me.
No sin-ner worse than I can be, There-fore I know He died for me.
Yet, since I know His grace is free, I know the Sav - ior died for me.

JOHN BAKEWELL.   SPANISH MELODY, FROM MARECHIO.

1. Hail, Thou once de-spis - ed Je - sus! Hail, Thou Gal - i - le - an King!
2. Pas-chal Lamb, by God ap-point - ed, All our sins on Thee were laid;
3. Je - sus, hail! en-throned in glo - ry, There for - ev - er to a - bide;
4. Wor-ship, hon - or, pow'r and bless-ing, Thou art worth - y to re - ceive;

Thou didst suf - fer to re - lease us; Thou didst free sal - va - tion bring.
By Al-might - y love a - noint-ed, Thou hast full a - tone-ment made.
All the heav'n - ly hosts a - dore Thee, Seat-ed at Thy Fa - ther's side:
Loud - est prais - es, with-out ceas - ing, Meet it is for us to give.

Hail, Thou ag - o - niz - ing Sav - ior, Bear-er of our sin and shame!
All Thy peo - ple are for - giv - en, Thro' the vir - tue of Thy blood;
There for sin - ners Thou art plead-ing; There Thou dost our place pre-pare;
Help, ye bright an-gel - ic Spir - its; Bring your sweet - est, no-blest lays;

By Thy mer - its we find fa - vor; Life is giv - en thro' Thy name.
O-pened is the gate of heav - en; Peace is made 'twixt man and God.
Ev - er for us in-ter-ced - ing, Till in glo - ry we ap-pear.
Help to sing our Sav-ior's mer - its; Help to chant Im-man-uel's praise!

No. 21.   Holy Cross.   C. M.

BERNARD OF CLAIRVAUX.
TR. BY E. CASWALL.

UNKNOWN.

1. Je - sus, the ver - y thought of Thee With sweet-ness fills the breast;
2. No voice can sing, no heart can frame, Nor can the mem - 'ry find
3. O hope of ev - 'ry con-trite heart, O joy of all the meek,
4. But what to those who find? Ah, this Nor tongue nor pen can show:
5. Je - sus, our on - ly joy be Thou, As Thou our prize wilt be;

But sweet - er far Thy face to see, And in Thy pres - ence rest.
A sweet - er sound than Je - sus' name, The Sav - ior of man-kind.
To those who ask, how kind Thou art! How good to those who seek!
The love of Je - sus, what it is, None but His loved ones know.
In Thee be all our glo - ry now, And thro' e - ter - ni - ty.

No. 22.   Arlington.   C. M.

ISAAC WATTS.

THOMAS AUGUSTINE ARNE.

1. Am I a sol - dier of the cross, A foll'wer of the Lamb,
2. Must I be car - ried to the skies On flow-'ry beds of ease,
3. Are there no foes for me to face? Must I not stem the flood?
4. Sure I must fight if I would reign; In-crease my cour - age, Lord;
5. Thy saints in all this glo-rious war Shall con-quer, tho' they die:
6. When that il - lus-trious day shall rise, And all Thy ar - mies shine

And shall I fear to own His cause, Or blush to speak His name?
While oth - ers fought to win the prize, And sailed thro' blood - y seas?
Is this vile world a friend to grace, To help me on to God?
I'll bear the toil, en - dure the pain, Sup - port - ed by Thy word.
They see the tri - umph from a - far, By faith they bring it nigh.
In robes of vic - t'ry thro' the skies, The glo - ry shall be Thine.

No. 23.   Missionary Chant. L. M.

H. KIRKE WHITE.   HEINRICH CHRISTOPHER ZEUNER.

1. When, marshaled on the night-ly plain, The glit-'ring host be-stud the sky,
2. Hark! hark! to God the chor-us breaks, From ev-'ry host, from ev-'ry gem;
3. Once on the rag-ing seas I rode, The storm was loud, the night was dark,
4. Deep hor-ror then my vi-tals froze; Death-struck, I ceased the tide to stem;
5. It was my guide, my light, my all, It bade my dark fore-bod-ings cease;
6. Now safe-ly moored, my per-ils o'er, I'll sing, first in night's di-a-dem,

One star a-lone of all the train Can fix the sin-ner's wan-d'ring eye.
But one a-lone the Sav-ior speaks, It is the Star of Beth-le-hem.
The o-cean yawned, and rude-ly blowed The wind that tossed my found'ring bark.
When sud-den-ly a star a-rose, It was the Star of Beth-le-hem.
And, thro' the storm and dan-ger's thrall, It led me to the port of peace.
For ev-er and for ev-er-more, The Star, the Star of Beth-le-hem.

No. 24.   Wilmot. 8, 7.

JOHN CAWOOD.   CARL MARIA von WEBER.

1. Hark! what mean those ho-ly voic-es, Sweet-ly sound-ing thro' the skies?
2. Lis-ten to the won-drous sto-ry, Which they chant in hymns of joy:
3. "Peace on earth, good-will from heav-en, Reach-ing far as man is found;
4. "Christ is born, the great A-noint-ed; Heav'n and earth His prais-es sing;
5. "Has-ten, mor-tals, to a-dore Him; Learn His name and taste His joy;

Lo! th'an-gel-ic host re-joic-es; Heav'n-ly hal-le-lu-jahs rise.
"Glo-ry in the high-est, glo-ry, Glo-ry be to God most high!
Souls re-deemed and sins for-giv-en! Loud our gold-en harps shall sound."
O, re-ceive whom God ap-point-ed, For your Pro-phet, Priest and King.
Till in heav'n ye sing be-fore Him; 'Glo-ry be to God most high!'"

No. 25.   Noel.   C. M.

JOHN G. WHITTIER.   LOWELL MASON.

1. We may not climb the heav'n-ly steeps To bring the Lord Christ down;
2. But warm, sweet, ten - der, ev - en yet A pres-ent help is He;
3. The heal - ing of the seam-less dress Is by our beds of pain;
4. Thro' Him the first fond pray'rs are said Our lips of child-hood frame;
5. O Lord and Mas - ter of us all, What-e'er our name or sign,

In vain we search the low - est deeps, For Him no depths can drown.
And faith has yet its Ol - i - vet, And love its Gal - i - lee.
We touch Him in life's throng and press, And we are whole a - gain.
The last low whis - pers of our dead Are bur-dened with His name.
We own Thy sway, we hear Thy call, We test our lives by Thine!

No. 26.   Eucharist.   L. M.

ISAAC WATTS.   ISAAC BAKER WOODBURY.

1. When I sur - vey the won-drous cross On which the Prince of glo - ry died,
2. For - bid it, Lord, that I should boast, Save in the death of Christ, my God;
3. See, from His head, His hands, His feet, Sor - row and love flow min-gled down:
4. Were the whole realm of na - ture mine, That were a pres - ent far too small;

My rich-est gain I count but loss, And pour con-tempt on all my pride.
All the vain things that charm me most, I sac - ri - fice them to His blood.
Did e'er such love and sor - row meet, Or thorns com-pose so rich a crown?
Love so a - maz - ing, so di - vine, De - mands my soul, my life, my all.

No. 27. Zion. 8, 7, 4.

WILLIAM WILLIAMS. THOMAS HASTINGS.

1. Guide me, O Thou great Je - ho - vah, Pil-grim thro' this bar-ren land: I am
2. O - pen now the crys-tal foun-tain, Whence the heal-ing wa-ters flow; Let the
3. When I tread the verge of Jor - dan, Bid my anx-ious fears sub-side; Bear me

weak, but Thou art might-y; Hold me with Thy pow'r-ful hand; Bread of heav-en,
fier - y, cloud-y pil - lar, Lead me all my jour-ney thro': Strong De-liv-'rer,
thro' the swell-ing cur - rent; Land me safe on Ca-naan's side: Songs of prais-es

Feed me till I want no more, Bread of heav-en, Feed me till I want no more.
Be Thou still my strength and shield, Strong Deliv'rer, Be Thou still my strength and shield.
I will ev - er give to Thee, Songs of prais-es I will ev - er give to Thee.

No. 28. Dennis. S. M.

JOHN FAWCETT. HANS GEORG NÄGELI.

1. Blest be the tie that binds Our hearts in Chris - tian love;
2. Be - fore our Fath - er's throne, We pour our ar - dent pray'rs;
3. We share our mu - tual woes, Our mu - tual bur - dens bear;
4. When we a - sun - der part; It gives us in - ward pain.

Dennis.

The fel - low - ship of kin - dred minds Is like to that a - bove.
Our fears, our hopes, our aims are one, Our com-forts and our cares.
And oft - en for each oth - er flows The sym - pa - thiz - ing tear.
But we shall still be joined in heart, And hope to meet a - gain.

No. 29. Selena. L. M. 61.

CHARLES WESLEY.   ISAAC BAKER WOODBURY.

1. O love di-vine, what hast Thou done! Th' in-car-nate God hath died for me!
2. Be-hold Him, all ye that pass by,—The bleeding Prince of life and peace!
3. Is cru - ci - fied for me and you, To bring us reb - els back to God:
4. Then let us sit be-neath His cross, And glad-ly catch the heal-ing stream;

The Fa-ther's co - e - ter-nal Son, Bore all my sins up - on the tree!
Come, sin-ners, see your Sav-ior die, And say, was ev - er grief like His?
Be-lieve, be-lieve the rec-ord true, Ye all are bought with Je-sus' blood;
All things for Him ac-count but loss, And give up all our hearts to Him:

The Son of God for me hath died: My Lord, my Love, is cru - ci - fied.
Come, feel with me His blood ap-plied: My Lord, my Love, is cru - ci - fied.
Par-don for all flows from His side: My Lord, my Love, is cru - ci - fied.
Of noth-ing think or speak be-side,—My Lord, my Love, is cru - ci - fied.

No. 30. Greenwood. S. M.

PAUL GERHARDT.

JOS. E. SWEETSER.

1. Since Je - sus is my friend, And I to Him be - long,
2. He whis-pers in my breast Sweet words of ho - ly cheer,
3. O, I would fix mine eyes On Christ, the Lord I love;

It mat-ters not what foes in - tend, How - ev - er fierce and strong.
How they who seek in God their rest Shall ev - er find Him near.
And sing for joy of that which lies Stored up for me a - bove.

No. 31. St. Martin's. C. M.

ISAAC WATTS.

WILLIAM TANSUR.

1. Come, Ho - ly Spir - it, heav'n-ly Dove, With all Thy quick'ning pow'rs;
2. Look how we grov - el here be - low, Fond of these earth - ly toys;
3. In vain we tune our form - al songs, In vain we strive to rise;
4. Fa - ther, and shall we ev - er live At this poor dy - ing rate,
5. Come, Ho - ly Spir - it, heav'n-ly Dove, With all Thy quick'ning pow'rs;

Kin - dle a flame of sa - cred love In these cold hearts of ours.
Our souls, how heav - i - ly they go, To reach e - ter - nal joys.
Ho - san - nas lan - guish on our tongues, And our de - vo - tion dies.
Our love so faint, so cold to Thee, And Thine to us so great?
Come, shed a - broad a Sav - ior's love, And that shall kin - dle ours.

No. 32.   Ware.   L. M.

NICOLAUS L. ZINZENDORF.
TR. BY J. WESLEY.

GEORGE KINGSLEY.

1. Je - sus, Thy blood and right-eous-ness My beau-ty are, my glo - rious dress;
2. Bold shall I stand in Thy great day, For who aught to my charge shall lay?
3. The ho - ly, meek, un-spot-ted Lamb, Who from the Fa-ther's bos - om came,
4. Lord, I be - lieve Thy pre-cious blood, Which, at the mer-cy - seat of God,
5. Lord, I be - lieve were sin-ners more Than sands up-on the o - cean shore,

'Midst flam-ing worlds, in these ar-rayed, With joy shall I lift up my head.
Ful - ly ab-solved thro' these I am, From sin and fear and guilt and shame.
Who died for me, e'en me to a-tone, Now for my Lord and God I own.
For - ev - er doth for sin-ners plead, For me, e'en for my soul, was shed.
Thou hast for all a ran-som paid, For all a full a - tone - ment made.

No. 33.   Cambridge.   C. M.

ISAAC WATTS.

JOHN RANDALL.

1. Sal - va-tion! O, the joy-ful sound! What pleasure to our ears! A sov'reign balm for
2. Sal - va-tion! let the ech - o fly The spa-cious earth a-round, While all the armies
3. Sal - va-tion! O Thou bleeding Lamb! To Thee the praise belongs; Salvation shall in-

ev-'ry wound, A cordial for our fears, A cordial for our fears, A cor-dial for our fears.
of the sky Conspire to raise the sound, Conspire to raise the sound, Conspire to raise the sound.
spire our hearts, And dwell upon our tongues, And dwell upon our tongues, And dwell upon our tongues.

No. 34.   Horton.   7.

Mrs. ANNA L. BARBAULD.

XAVIER SCHNYDER von WARTENSEE.

1. Come, said Je - sus' sa - cred voice,   Come, and make my paths your choice;
2. Thou who, house-less, sole, for-lorn,   Long hast borne the proud world's scorn,
3. Ye who, tossed on beds of pain,   Seek for ease, but seek in vain;
4. Hith - er come, for here is found   Balm that flows for ev - 'ry wound,

    I will guide you to your home;   Wea - ry pil - grim, hith - er come.
Long hast roamed the bar - ren waste,   Wea - ry pil - grim, hith - er haste.
Ye, by fierc - er an - guish torn,   In re-morse for guilt who mourn;
Peace that ev - er shall en - dure,   Rest e - ter - nal, sa-cred, sure.

No. 35.   Pleyel's Hymn.   7.

THOMAS SCOTT.

IGNACE PLEYEL.

1. Hast - en, sin - ner, to be wise!   Stay not for the mor-row's sun:
2. Hast - en, mer - cy to im - plore!   Stay not for the mor-row's sun,
3. Hast - en, sin - ner, to re - turn!   Stay not for the mor-row's sun,
4. Hast - en, sin - ner, to be blest!   Stay not for the mor-row's sun,

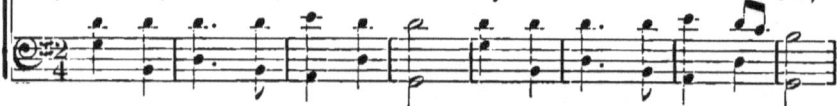

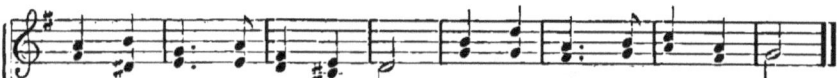

Wis - dom if you still de - spise,   Hard - er is it to be won.
Lest thy sea - son should be o'er   Ere this ev - 'ning's stage be run.
Lest thy lamp should fail to burn   Ere sal - va - tion's work is done.
Lest per - di - tion thee ar - rest   Ere the mor - row is be - gun.

No. 36. Ingham. L. M.

GERHARD TERSTEEGEN.
TR. BY MISS J. BORTHWICK.

LOWELL MASON.

1. God call-ing yet! shall I not hear? Earth's pleasures shall I still hold dear?
2. God call-ing yet! shall I not rise? Can I His lov - ing voice de-spise,
3. God call-ing yet! and shall He knock, And I my heart the clos - er lock?
4. God call-ing yet! and shall I give No heed, but still in bond-age live?
5. God call-ing yet! I can - not stay; My heart I yield with-out de - lay:

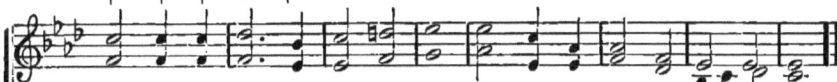

Shall life's swift pass-ing years all fly, And still my soul in slum-ber lie?
And base-ly His kind care re - pay! He 'calls me still; can I de - lay?
He still is wait - ing to re-ceive, And shall I dare His Spir-it grieve?
I wait, but He does not for-sake; He calls me still; my heart, a - wake!
Vain world, fare-well, from thee I part; The voice of God hath reached my heart.

No. 37. Heber. C. M.

ISAAC WATTS.

GEORGE KINGSLEY.

1. With joy we med - i - tate the grace Of our High Priest a - bove;
2. Touched with a sym - pa - thy with - in, He knows our fee - ble frame;
3. He, in the days of fee - ble flesh, Poured out strong cries and tears,
4. He'll nev - er quench the smok-ing flax, But raise it to a flame;
5. Then let our hum - ble faith ad-dress His mer - cy and His pow'r;

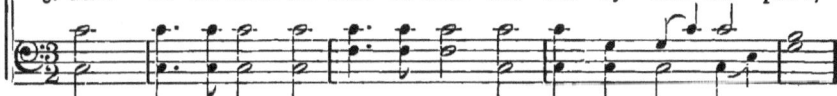

His heart is made of ten-der-ness, His bow-els melt with love.
He knows what sore temp - ta-tions mean, For He hath felt the same.
And in His meas-ure feels a-fresh What ev -'ry mem - ber bears.
The bruis - ed reed He nev - er breaks, Nor scorns the mean-est name.
We shall ob - tain de - liv-'ring grace In ev -'ry try - ing hour.

Coronation. C. M.

EDWARD PERRONET. ALT.   OLIVER HOLDEN.

1. All hail the pow'r of Je - sus' name! Let an - gels pros-trate fall;
2. Crown Him, ye morn - ing stars of light, Who fixed this earth - ly ball;
3. Ye chos - en seed of Is - rael's race, Ye ran-somed from the fall,
4. Sin - ners, whose love can ne'er for - get The worm-wood and the gall;
5. Let ev - 'ry kin-dred, ev - 'ry tribe, On this ter - res - trial ball,
6. O, that with yon - der sa - cred throng We at His feet may fall!

Bring forth the roy - al di - a - dem, And crown Him Lord of all,
Now hail the strength of Is - rael's might, And crown Him Lord of all,
Hail Him who saves you by His grace, And crown Him Lord of all,
Go, spread your tro-phies at His feet, And crown Him Lord of all,
To Him all maj - es - ty as - cribe, And crown Him Lord of all,
We'll join the ev - er - last-ing song, And crown Him Lord of all,

Bring forth the roy - al di - a - dem, And crown Him Lord of all.
Now hail the strength of Is - rael's might, And crown Him Lord of all.
Hail Him who saves you by His grace, And crown Him Lord of all.
Go, spread your tro-phies at His feet, And crown Him Lord of all.
To Him all maj - es - ty as - cribe, And crown Him Lord of all.
We'll join the ev - er - last- ing song, And crown Him Lord of all.

No. 39.   Seymour. L. M.

PSALM 126.   W. B. BRADBURY.

1. 'Twas like a dream, when by the Lord From bond-age Zi - on was re-stored:
2. The heathen owned what God had wrought; Great works, which joy to us have bro't,
3. Who sows in tears, with joy shall reap; Tho' bear-ing pre - cious seed they weep

Seymour.

Ritard.

Our mouths were filled with mirth, our tongues Were ev - er sing-ing joy-ful songs.
As South-ern streams, when filled with rain, Lord, turn our cap-tive state a-gain.
While go - ing forth, yet shall they sing, When coming back their sheaves they bring.

No. 40. Anvern. L. M.

PSALM 14.   ARR. BY DR. L. MASON.

1. The God who sits en-throned on high The fool doth in his heart de-
2. From heav'n with search-ing eye the Lord Did all the sons of men re-
3. From right-eous ways they all de - part; All are cor-rupt and vile. in
4. Has know-ledge from the wick - ed fled, That they my peo - ple eat as
5. There fear-ful ter - ror on them fell; For God doth with the right-eous
6. May Is - rael's help from Zi - on come; When God shall bring His cap-tives

ny; Cor - rupt are they, vile works have done, And do - ing
gard: To see if a - ny un - der - stood, If a - ny
heart; A - mong them do - ing good is none, A - mong them
bread? That they de - light in works of shame, And call not
dwell; The poor man's coun - sel you de - spise, Be - cause in
home, Then Ja - cob great - ly shall re - joice, And Is - rael

Ritard.

good there is not one, And do-ing good there is not one.
one were seek - ing God, If a - ny one were seek - ing God.
all, not. ev - en one, A-mong them all, not ev - en one.
on Je - ho - vah's name? And call not on Je - ho - vah's name?
God His ref - uge lies, Be-cause in God his ref - uge lies.
shout with glad - some voice, And Is-rael shout with glad - some voice.

No. 41.   Belmont.   C. M.

PHILIP DODDRIDGE.   SAMUEL WEBBE.

1. A-wake, my soul, stretch ev - 'ry nerve, And press with vig - or on;
2. A cloud of wit - ness-es a - round Hold thee in full sur - vey;
3. 'Tis God's all - an - i - mat - ing voice That calls thee from on high;
4. Then wake, my soul, stretch ev - 'ry nerve, And press with vig - or on;

A heav'n-ly race de - mands thy zeal, And an im - mor - tal crown.
For - get the steps al - read - y trod, And on - ward urge thy way.
'Tis His own hand pre - sents the prize To Thine as - pir - ing eye.
A heav'n-ly race de - mands thy zeal, And an im - mor - tal crown.

No. 42.   Hermon.   C. M.

JOSEPH SWAIN.   LOWELL MASON.

1. How sweet, how heav'n-ly is the sight, When those who love the Lord
2. When each can feel his broth-er's sigh, And with him bear a part!
3. When, free from en - vy, scorn, and pride, Our wish-es all a - bove,
4. Let love, in one de-light-ful stream, Thro' ev-'ry bos - om flow,
5. Love is the gold-en chain that binds The hap-py souls a - bove;

In one an - oth - er's peace de-light, And so ful - fill His word!
When sor - row flows from eye to eye, And joy from heart to heart!
Each can his broth - er's fail-ings hide, And show a broth - er's lovel
And un - ion sweet, and dear es-teem, In ev - 'ry ac - tion glow.
And he's an heir of heav'n who finds His bos-om glow with love.

No. 43.   Avon.   C. M.

CHARLES WESLEY.

HUGH WILSON.

1. For - ev - er here   my rest shall be,   Close to   Thy bleed-ing   side;
2. My   dy - ing Sav - ior, and   my God,   Foun-tain   for guilt and   sin,
3. Wash me, and make me thus Thine own; Wash me,   and mine Thou art;
4. Th'a-tone-ment of   Thy blood ap - ply,   Till faith   to sight im-prove;

This all   my hope, and all   my plea,   "For   me   the Sav - ior died."
Sprink-le   me ev - er with Thy blood,   And cleanse and keep me clean.
Wash me,   but not   my feet   a - lone,   My hands,   my head, my heart.
Till hope   in full   fru - i - tion die,   And all   my soul   be love.

No. 44.   St. Agnes.   C. M.

FREDERICK W. FABER.

REV. JOHN BACCHUS DYKES.

1. O   it is   hard   to   work for God,   To rise and take   His   part
2. He hides him - self   so   won-drous-ly,   As tho' there were   no   God;
3. Or He de - serts   us   in   the hour   The fight is   all   but   lost;
4. It   is not   so,   but   so   it looks;   And we lose cour - age   then;
5. But right is   right, since God   is God;   And right the day   must win;

Up - on this   bat - tle - field   of earth,   And not some-times lose heart!
He   is least seen   when   all   the pow'rs   Of   ill are most   a - broad.
And seems to   leave   us   to   our - selves   Just when we need   Him most.
And doubts will come   if   God hath kept   His prom-is - es   to   men.
To doubt would be   dis - loy - al - ty,   To fal - ter would be   sin!

No. 45. Onward. 6. 5.

SABINE BARING-GOULD.

Sir ARTHUR SEYMOUR SULLIVAN.

1. On-ward, Christian sol-diers! March-ing as to war, With the cross of Je - sus
2. At the sign of tri - umph Sa-tan's host doth flee; On, then, Christian sol-diers,
3. Like a might-y ar - my Moves the Church of God; Brothers, we are tread-ing
4. Crowns and thrones may perish, Kingdoms rise and wane, But the Church of Je-sus
5. On-ward, then, ye peo - ple! Join our hap-py throng, Blend with ours your voic-es

Go - ing on be-fore. Christ, the roy - al Mas - ter, Leads a-gainst the foe;
On to vic - to - ry! Hell's foun-da-tions quiv - er At the shout of praise;
Where the saints have trod; We are not di - vid - ed, All one bod - y we,
Con-stant will re-main; Gates of hell can nev - er 'Gainst the Church pre-vail;
In the tri-umph-song; Glo-ry, laud and hon - or Un - to Christ the King,

For-ward in - to bat - tle, See, His ban-ners go! Onward, Christian sol - diers!
Brothers, lift your voic-es, Loud your anthems raise. Onward, Christian sol - diers!
One in hope and doc-trine, One in char - i - ty. Onward, Christian sol - diers!
We have Christ's own promise, And that cannot fail. Onward, Christian sol - diers!
This thro' count-less a - ges Men and an-gels sing. Onward, Christian sol - diers!

March-ing as to war, With the cross of Je - sus Go-ing on be-fore.

No. 46.   Illinois.   L. M.

JOHN G. WHITTIER.

REV. JONATHAN SPILMAN.
ARR. BY THOMAS HASTINGS.

1. It may not be our lot to wield The sick-le in the rip-ened field;
2. Yet where our du-ty's task is wrought In u - ni-son with God's great tho't,
3. And ours the grate-ful serv-ice whence Comes, day by day, the rec-om-pense;
4. And were this life the ut-most span, The on - ly end and aim of man,
5. But life, tho' fall-ing like our grain, Like that re-vives and springs a-gain;

Nor ours to hear, on Sum-mer eves, The reap-er's song a-mong the sheaves.
The near and fu-ture blend in one, And what-so - e'er is willed, is done.
The hope, the trust, the pur-pose stayed, The foun-tain and the noon-day shade.
Bet - ter the toil of fields like these, Than wak-ing dream and sloth-ful ease.
And, ear - ly called, how blest are they Who wait in heav'n their har-vest day!

No. 47.   Retreat.   L. M.

HUGH STOWELL.

THOMAS HASTINGS.

1. From ev - 'ry storm-y wind that blows, From ev - 'ry swell-ing tide of woes,
2. There is a place where Je - sus sheds The oil of glad-ness on our heads;
3. There is a scene where spir - its blend, Where friend holds fellowship with friend:
4. There, there on ea - gle wings we soar, And sin and sense mo-lest no more;

There is a calm, a sure re-treat: 'Tis found be-neath the mer - cy - seat.
A place than all be-sides more sweet: It is the blood-bought mer-cy - seat.
Tho' sun-dered far, by faith they meet A-round one com-mon mer - cy - seat.
And heav'n comes down our souls to greet, While glo - ry crowns the mer - cy - seat.

No. 48. Toplady. 7, 61.

AUGUSTUS M. TOPLADY. ALT.   THOMAS HASTINGS.

1. Rock of a - ges, cleft for me, Let me hide my - self in Thee;
2. Could my tears for - ev - er flow, Could my zeal no lan - guor know,
3. While I draw this fleet - ing breath, When my eyes shall close in death,

Let the wa - ter and the blood, From Thy wound-ed side which flowed,
These for sin could not a - tone; Thou must save, and Thou a - lone:
When I rise to worlds un-known, And be - hold Thee on Thy throne,

Be of sin the doub - le cure, Save from wrath and make me pure.
In my hand no price I bring; Sim - ply to Thy cross I cling.
Rock of a - ges, cleft for me, Let me hide my - self in Thee.

No. 49. Woodworth. L. M.

CHARLOTTE ELLIOTT.   WILLIAM BATCHELDER BRADBURY.

1. Just as I am, with-out one plea, But that Thy blood was shed for me,
2. Just as I am, and wait-ing not To rid my soul of one dark blot,
3. Just as I am, tho' tossed a - bout With many a con-flict, many a doubt,
4. Just as I am—poor, wretched, blind; Sight, rich-es, heal-ing of the mind,
5. Just as I am—Thou wilt re-ceive, Wilt wel-come, par-don, cleanse, relieve;
6. Just as I am—Thy love un-known Hath bro-ken ev - 'ry bar-rier down;

Woodworth.

And that Thou bidst me come to Thee, O Lamb of God, I come! I come!
To Thee whose blood can cleanse each spot, O Lamb of God, I come! I come!
Fight-ings with-in, and fears with-out, O Lamb of God, I come! I come!
Yea, all I need, in Thee to find, O Lamb of God, I come! I come!
Be-cause Thy prom-ise I be-lieve, O Lamb of God, I come! I come!
Now, to be Thine, yea, Thine a-lone, O Lamb of God, I come! I come!

No. 50. Lenox. H. M.

CHAS. WESLEY.

LEWIS EDSON.

1. Blow ye the trum-pet, blow; The glad-ly sol-emn sound Let all the
2. Ex - tol the Lamb of God, The all - a - ton-ing Lamb; Re - demp-tion
3. Ye who have sold for naught Your her - i - tage a - bove, Come, take it
4. The gos - pel trump-et hear, The news of heav'n-ly grace, And saved from

na-tions know, To earth's re-mot-est bound; The year of Ju - bi - lee is come:
in His blood Throughout the world proclaim. The year of Ju - bi - lee is come:
back un-bought, The gift of Je-sus' love. The year of Ju - bi - lee is come:
earth ap-pear Be - fore your Sav-ior's face. The year of Ju - bi - lee is come:

Re-turn, ye ran-somed sinners, home, Re-turn, ye ran-somed sin - ners, home.

No. 51.   Paradise. 8, 6, 6.

FREDERICK W. FABER.   JOSEPH BARNBY.

1. O par - a - dise! O par - a - dise! Who doth not crave for rest?
2. O par - a - dise! O par - a - dise! The world is grow-ing old;
3. O par - a - dise! O par - a - dise! 'Tis wea - ry wait-ing here;
4. O par - a - dise! O par - a - dise! I want to sin no more,
5. O par - a - dise! O par - a - dise! I great - ly long to see

Who would not seek the hap - py land Where they that loved are blest;
Who would not be at rest and free Where love is nev - er cold;
I long to be where Je - sus is, To feel, to see Him near;
I want to be as pure on earth As on Thy spot - less shore;
The spec - ial place my dear - est Lord In love pre-pares for me;

Where loy - al hearts and true

Where loy - - al hearts and true Stand ev - er in the light,

All rap - ture through and through, In God's most ho - ly sight?

No. 52.   Clarendon. C. M.

R. HEBER.

1. The Son of God goes forth to war, A king - ly crown to gain;
2. Who best can drink his cup of woe, Tri - umph-ant o - ver pain;
3. A no - ble ar - my: men and boys, The ma - tron and the maid;
4. They climbed the steep as-cent of heav'n Thro per - il, toil, and pain:

His blood-red ban - ner streams a - far: Who fol - lows in His train?
Who pa-tient bears his cross be - low, He fol - lows in His train.
A - round the Sav - ior's throne re - joice, In robes of light ar - rayed.
O God, to us may grace be giv'n To fol - low in their train.

No. 53.   Naomi. C. M.

ANNE STEELE.   HANS GEORG NÄGELI

1. Fa - ther, what-e'er of earth - ly bliss Thy sov-'reign will de - nies,
2. Give me a calm, a thank-ful heart, From ev - 'ry mur-mur free;
3. Let the sweet hope that Thou art mine My life and death at - tend;

Ac - cept - ed at Thy throne of grace, Let this pe - ti - tion rise:
The bless-ings of Thy grace im - part, And make me live to Thee.
Thy pres-ence thro' my jour - ney shine, And crown my jour - ney's end.

No. 54.   Olivet. 6, 4.

RAY PALMER.   LOWELL MASON.

1. My faith looks up to Thee, Thou Lamb of Cal - va - ry,
2. May Thy rich grace im-part Strength to my faint - ing heart,
3. While life's dark maze I tread, And griefs a - round me spread,
4. When ends life's tran - sient dream, When death's cold, sul - len stream

Sav - ior di - vine! Now hear me while I pray; Take all my
My zeal in - spire! As Thou hast died for me, O, may my
Be Thou my Guide; Bid dark-ness turn to day, Wipe sor - row's
Shall o'er me roll, Blest Sav - ior, then, in love, Fear and dis-

guilt a - way; O, let me from this day Be whol - ly Thine!
love to Thee Pure, warm, and change-less be— A liv - ing fire!
tears a - way, Nor let me ev - er stray From Thee a - side.
trust re-move; O, bear me safe a - bove—A ran - somed soul.

No. 55.   Badea. S. M.

CHARLES WESLEY.   GERMAN MELODY.

1. How can a sin - ner know His sins on earth for - giv'n?
2. What we have felt and seen With con - fi - dence we tell;
3. We who in Christ be - lieve That He for us hath died,
4. Ex - ults our ris - ing soul, Dis - bur - dened of her load,
5. His love, sur - pass - ing far The love of all be - neath,
6. Strong - er than death or hell The sa - cred pow'r we prove;

Badea.

How can my gra-cious Sav-ior show My name in-scribed in heav'n?
And pub-lish to the sons of men The sign in-fal-li-ble.
We all His un-known peace re-ceive, And feel His blood ap-plied.
And swells un-ut-ter-a-bly full Of glo-ry and of God.
We find with-in our hearts, and dare The point-less darts of death.
And, conq-'rers of the world, we dwell In heav'n, who dwell in love.

No. 56. **Bread of Life.** **10.**

MARY A. LATHBURY.   WM. F. SHERWIN.

1. Break Thou the bread of life, dear Lord, to me, As Thou didst
2. Bless Thou the pre-cious truth, dear Lord, to me, As Thou didst

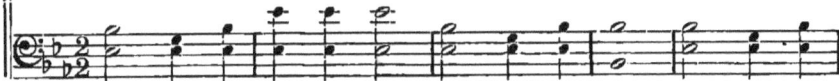

break the loaves be-side the sea; Be-yond the sa-cred page
bless the bread by Gal-i-lee; Then shall all bond-age cease,

I seek Thee, Lord; My spir-it pants for Thee, O, liv-ing Word!
all fet-ters fall, And I shall find my peace, my all in all!

Copyright, 1877, by J. H. Vincent. Used by permission.

No. 57.   Aurelia. 7, 6. D.

SAMUEL JOHN STONE.

SAMUEL SEBASTIAN WESLEY.

1. The Church's one foun-da - tion Is Je - sus Christ her Lord; She is His new cre-
2. E - lect from ev - 'ry na - tion, Yet one o'er all the earth, Her char-ter of sal-
3. Yet she on earth hath un - ion With God the Three in One, And mystic sweet com-

a - tion By wa - ter and the word: From heav'n He came and sought her To
va - tion One Lord, one faith, one birth; One Ho - ly Name she bless - es, Par-
mun - ion With those whose rest is won: O, hap-py ones and ho - ly! Lord,

be His ho - ly bride; With His own blood He bought her, And for her life He died.
takes one ho - ly food, And to one hope she press - es, With ev - 'ry grace en-dued.
give us grace that we Like them, the meek and low-ly, On high may dwell with Thee.

No. 58.   Boylston. S. M.

CHARLES WESLEY.

LOWELL MASON.

1. A charge to keep I have, A God to glo - ri - fy;
2. To serve the pres - ent age, My call - ing to ful - fill,—
3. Arm me with jeal - ous care, As in Thy sight to live;
4. Help me to watch and pray, And on Thy - self re - ly,

Boylston.

A nev - er - dy - ing soul to save, And fit it for the sky.
O, may it all my pow'rs en - gage, To do my Mas - ter's will.
And O, Thy serv - ant, Lord, pre - pare, A strict ac-count to give.
As - sured, if I my trust be - tray, I shall for - ev - er die.

No. 59. Selvin. S. M.

AUGUSTUS M. TOPLADY.

GERMAN.
ARR. BY LOWELL MASON.

1. If, on a qui - et sea, Toward heav'n we calm-ly sail,
2. But should the surg - es rise, And rest de - lay to come,
3. Soon shall our doubts and fears All yield to Thy con-trol;
4. Teach us in ev - 'ry state, To make Thy will our own;

With grate-ful hearts, O God, to Thee, We'll own the fav - 'ring gale,
Blest be the tem - pest, kind the storm, Which drives us near - er home,
Thy ten-der mer - cies shall il - lume The mid-night of the soul,
And when the joys of sense de - part, To live by faith a - lone,

With grate-ful hearts, O God, to Thee, We'll own the fav - 'ring gale.
Blest be the tem - pest, kind the storm, Which drives us near - er home.
Thy ten-der mer - cies shall il - lume The mid-night of the soul.
And when the joys of sense de - part, To live by faith a - lone.

No. 60.   Jewett.   6.

BENJAMIN SCHMOLKE.
TR. BY MISS J. BORTHWICK.

CARL MARIA WEBER
ARR. BY J. P. HOLBROOK.

1. My Je - sus, as Thou wilt: O, may Thy will be mine; In - to Thy
2. My Je - sus, as Thou wilt: Tho' seen thro' many a tear, Let not my
3. My Je - sus, as Thou wilt: All shall be well for me; Each chang-ing

hand of love I would my all re - sign. Thro' sor - row or thro' joy,
star of hope Grow dim or dis-ap - pear. Since Thou on earth hast wept
fu - ture scene I glad - ly trust with Thee. Straight to my home a - bove,

Con-duct me as Thine own, And help me still to say, "My Lord, Thy will be done."
And sor-rowed oft a-lone, If I must weep with Thee, My Lord, Thy will be done.
I trav-el calm-ly on, And sing in life or death, "My Lord, Thy will be done."

No. 61.   Rockingham.   L. M.

PSALM 22 : 22.

DR. LOWELL MASON.

1. I will to breth-ren show Thy name, With-in the Church Thy praise pro-claim;
2. For He de-spised not, nor ab-horred Those who in trou - ble sought the Lord;
3. To Thee in praise I'll lift my song, A - mid the great as - sem-bled throng;
4. The meek shall eat till sat - is - fied, The food Thy lib - 'ral hands pro-vide.

Rockingham.

Who fear the Lord, Him laud and praise, Him fear, all ye of Ja-cob's race.
He nev-er turns His face a-way, But hears the hum-ble when they pray.
Where those who fear Je-ho-vah bow, I will per-form my sa-cred vow.
Who seek the Lord, shall Him a-dore; Your heart shall live for ev-er-more.

No. 62.   Come, Ye Disconsolate.   11, 10.

THOMAS MOORE.   SAMUEL WEBBE.

1. Come, ye dis-con-so-late, wher-e'er ye lan-guish; Come to the
2. Joy of the des-o-late, light of the stray-ing, Hope of the
3. Here see the bread of life; see wa-ters flow-ing Forth from the

mer-cy-seat, fer-vent-ly kneel; Here bring your wound-ed hearts,
pen-i-tent, fade-less and pure, Here speaks the Com-fort-er,
throne of God, pure from a-bove; Come to the feast of love;

here tell your an-guish; Earth has no sor-row that heav'n can-not heal.
ten-der-ly say-ing, "Earth has no sor-row that heav'n can-not cure."
come, ev-er know-ing Earth has no sor-row but heav'n can remove.

No. 63.   Henley.   11, 10.

MRS. CATHERINE H. ESLING.   LOWELL MASON.

1. Come un - to me, when shad-ows dark-ly gath - er, When the sad
2. Large are the man - sions in thy Fa-ther's dwell - ing, Glad are the
3. There, like an E - den blos-som-ing in glad - ness, Bloom the fair

heart is wea - ry and dis - tressed, Seek - ing for com - fort
homes that sor - rows nev - er dim; Sweet are the harps in
flow'rs the earth too rude - ly pressed; Come un - to me, all

from your heav'n-ly Fa - ther, Come un - to me, and I will give you rest.
ho - ly mu - sic swell-ing, Soft are the tones which raise the heav'n-ly hymn.
ye who droop in sad - ness, Come un - to me, and I will give you rest.

No. 64.   Olmutz.   S. M.

AUGUSTUS M. TOPLADY.   GREGORIAN CHANT.
ALT. BY B. W. NOEL.   ARR. BY LOWELL MASON.

1. Your harps, ye trem - bling saints, Down from the wil - lows take;
2. Tho' in a for - eign land, We are not far from home;
3. His grace will to the end Strong - er and bright - er shine:
4. When we in dark - ness walk, Nor feel the heav'n - ly flame,
5. Soon shall our doubts and fears Sub - side at His con - trol;
6. Blest is the man, O God, That stays him - self on Thee;

Olmutz.

Loud   to the praise of   love di-vine   Bid   ev-'ry string   a - wake.
And   near-er to   our   house a - bove   We   ev-'ry mo - ment come.
Nor   pres-ent things, nor   things to come, Shall quench the spark di - vine.
Then   is the time   to   trust our God,   And   rest up - on   His name.
His   lov-ing-kind - ness shall break thro'   The   mid-night of   the soul.
Who   waits for Thy   sal - va-tion, Lord,   Shall Thy sal - va - tion see.

No. 65.   Bethany. 6, 4, 6,

Mrs. SARAH F. ADAMS.   LOWELL MASON.

1. Near - er, my God, to Thee! Near-er to Thee, E'en tho' it   be   a cross
2. Tho' like   a wan - der - er, The sun gone down, Dark-ness be   o - ver me,
3. There let   the way ap-pear, Steps un - to heav'n; All that Thou send-est me,
4. Then, with my wak - ing tho'ts Bright with Thy praise, Out of my ston - y griefs
5. Or   if,   on joy - ful wing Cleav-ing the sky,   Sun, moon and stars for-got,

That   rais - eth me;   Still   all my song shall be,   Near - er, my
My   rest   a stone,   Yet   in my dreams I'd be,   Near - er, my
In   mer - cy giv'n;   An - gels to beck - on me   Near - er, my
Beth - el I'll raise;   So   by my woes to be,   Near - er, my
Up - ward I fly,   Still   all my song shall be,   Near - er, my

God, to Thee, Near - er, my God, to Thee, Near - er to Thee!

No. 66. What a Friend we Have in Jesus. 8, 7. D.

H. BONAR.

C. C. CONVERSE.

1. What a Friend we have in Je - sus, All our sins and griefs to bear!
2. Have we tri - als and temp-ta - tions? Is there trou-ble a - ny-where?
3. Are we weak and heav-y la - den, Cum-bered with a load of care?

What a priv - i - lege to car - ry Ev - 'ry thing to God in pray'r!
We should nev - er be dis-cour - aged, Take it to the Lord in pray'r.
Pre - cious Sav-ior, still our ref - uge,— Take it to the Lord in pray'r.

O, what peace we oft - en for - feit, O, what need-less pain we bear,
Can we find a friend so faith - ful Who will all our sor-rows share?
Do thy friends de-spise, for-sake thee? Take it to the Lord in pray'r;

All be-cause we do not car - ry Ev - 'ry thing to God in pray'r!
Je - sus knows our ev - 'ry weak - ness, Take it to the Lord in pray'r.
In His arms He'll take and shield Thee, Thou wilt find a so - lace there.

No. 67.   Maitland.   C. M.

THOMAS SHEPHERD. ALT.   GEO. N. ALLEN.

1. Must Je - sus bear the cross a - lone, And all the world go free?
2. How hap - py are the saints a - bove, Who once went sorrowing here!
3. The con - se - crat - ed cross I'll bear, Till death shall set me free;

No, there's a cross for ev - 'ry one, And there's a cross for me.
But now they taste un - min - gled love, And joy with - out a tear.
And then go home my crown to wear, For there's a crown for me.

No. 68.   Leighton.   S. M.

MARY B. TOUCEY.   GREATOREX.

1. Sow, ere the eve-ning falls, The seed with - in thy hand,
2. Sow heart - felt deeds and pray'rs, Nor ques - tion where they lie;
3. Sow with no self - ish aim, For soon the time will come.
4. Sow all in faith and love; Tho' late the glean - ing be,

A - long the fur - rows at thy feet, Or broad-cast o'er the land.
As-sured that not the small - est one Es-capes the Mas - ter's eye.
When He who sifts the chaff from wheat, Will call His har - vest home.
How sweet to hear Him say at last, "Ye did it un - to me."

No. 69.   Welton. L. M.

BERNARD of CLAIRVAUX.
TR. BY RAY PALMER.

FROM REV. ABRAHAM HENRI CÆSAR MALAN.

1. Je - sus, Thou Joy of lov - ing hearts! Thou Fount of life! Thou Light of men!
2. Thy truth un-changed hath ev-er stood; Thou sav-est those that on Thee call;
3. We taste Thee, O Thou Liv-ing Bread, And long to feast up - on Thee still;
4. Our rest-less spir - its yearn for Thee, Where'er our change-ful lot is cast;
5. O Je - sus, ev - er with us stay; Make all our mo-ments calm and bright;

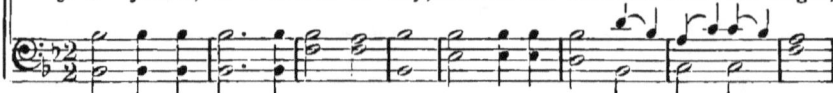

From the best bliss that earth im-parts, We turn un-filled to Thee a - gain.
To them that seek Thee, Thou art good, To them that find Thee, all in all.
We drink of Thee, the Foun-tain Head, And thirst our souls from Thee to fill!
Glad, when Thy gra-cious smile we see, Blest, when our faith can hold Thee fast.
Chase the dark night of sin a - way, Shed o'er the world Thy ho - ly light!

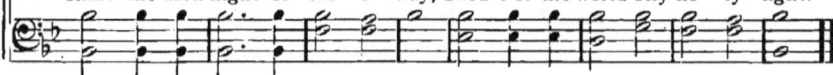

No. 70.   Emmons. C. M.

JOHN CENNICK.

ARR. FROM FRIEDRICH BURGMÜLLER.

1. Thou dear Re-deem-er, dy-ing Lamb, I love to hear of Thee; No mu - sic's
2. O, let me ev - er hear Thy voice In mer - cy to me speak; In Thee, my
3. My Je - sus shall be still my theme, While in this world I stay; I'll sing my
4. When I ap-pear in yon-der cloud, With all Thy fav-ored throng, Then will I

like Thy charming name, Nor half so sweet can be, Nor half so sweet can be.
Priest, will I re-joice, And Thy sal - va - tion seek, And Thy sal - va - tion seek.
Je - sus' love-ly name When all things else de-cay, When all things else de-cay.
sing more sweet, more loud, And Christ shall be my song, And Christ shall be my song.

No. 71.   Hendon.   7.

JOHN CENNICK.   Rev. ABRAHAM HENRI CÆSAR MALAN.

1. Chil-dren of the heav'nly king, As we jour-ney let us sing; Sing our Sav-ior's
2. We are trav-'ling home to God, In the way our fa-thers trod; They are hap-py
3. O, ye ban-ished seed, be glad; Christ our Ad-vo-cate is made: Us to save our
4. Fear not, breth-ren, joy-ful stand On the bor-ders of our land; Je-sus Christ, our
5. Lord, o - be - dient-ly we'll go, Glad-ly leav-ing all be - low: On - ly Thou our

wor-thy praise, Glo-rious in His works and ways, Glo-rious in His works and ways.
now, and we Soon their hap-pi - ness shall see, Soon their hap-pi - ness shall see.
flesh as - sumes, Broth-er to our souls be - comes, Broth-er to our souls be-comes.
Fa-ther's Son, Bids us un - dis-mayed go on, Bids us un - dis-mayed go on.
Lead-er be, And we still will fol - low Thee, And we still will fol - low Thee.

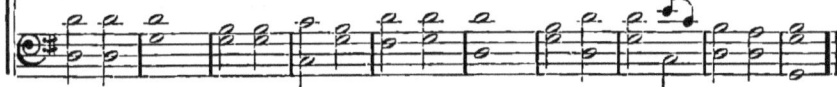

No. 72.   Wellesley.   8, 7.

FREDERICK W. FABER.   LIZZIE S. TOURJEE.

1. There's a wide-ness in God's mer - cy, Like the wide - ness of the sea,
2. There is wel - come for the sin - ner, And more gra - ces for the good,
3. For the love of God is broad-er Than the meas-ure of man's mind;
4. If our love were but more sim - ple, We should take Him at His word;

There's a kind - ness in His jus - tice, Which is more than lib - er - ty.
There is mer - cy with the Sav - ior; There is heal - ing in His blood.
And the heart of the E - ter - nal, Is most won - der - ful - ly kind.
And our lives would be all sun-shine In the sweet-ness of our Lord.

No. 73.   Missionary Hymn.   7, 6.

REGINALD HEBER.   LOWELL MASON.

1. From Green-land's i - cy mountains, From India's coral strand; Where Afric's sun-ny
2. What tho' the spi - cy breez - es Blow soft o'er Cey-lon's isle; Tho' ev-'ry pros-pect
3. Shall we, whose souls are light-ed With wisdom from on high, Shall we to men be-
4. Waft, waft, ye winds, His sto - ry, And you, ye wa-ters, roll, Till, like a sea of

foun-tains Roll down their gold-en sand; From many an an-cient riv - er, From
pleas - es, And on - ly man is vile? In vain with lav - ish kind - ness The
night - ed The lamp of life de - ny? Sal - va-tion! O sal-va - tion! The
glo - ry, It spreads from pole to pole: Till o'er our ran-somed na - ture The

many a palm-y plain, They call us to de - liv - er Their land from er-ror's chain.
gifts of God are strown; The heathen in his blindness Bows down to wood and stone.
joy-ful sound pro-claim, Till earth's remotest na-tion Has learned Messiah's name.
Lamb for sin-ners slain, Re-deem-er, King, Cre-a-tor, In bliss re-turns to reign.

No. 74.   Now the Day is Over.

SABINE BARING-GOULD.   J. BARNBY.

1. Now the day is o - ver, Night is draw - ing nigh,
2. Now the dark - ness gath - ers, Stars be - gin to peep,
3. Je - sus, give the wea - ry Calm and sweet re - pose,
4. Thro' the long night watch - es May Thine an - gels spread
5. When the morn - ing wak - ens, Then may I a - rise
6. Glo - ry to the Fa - ther, Glo - ry to the Son,

Now the Day is Over.

Shad-ows of the ev - 'ning — Steal a - cross the sky.
Birds and beasts, and flow - ers — Soon will be a - sleep.
With Thy ten-d'rest bless - ing, — May our eye - lids close.
Their white wings a - bove me, — Watch-ing round my bed.
Pure and fresh and sin - less — In Thy ho - ly eyes.
And to Thee, blest Spir - it, — Whilst all a - ges run. — A - men.

ev-'ning steal a-cross the sky.

No. 75. Lischer. H. M.

LOWELL MASON.

1. Wel-come, de-light-ful morn, Thou day of sa - cred rest; We hail thy kind re-
2. Now may the Lord de-scend And fill His throne of grace, Thy scep-ter, Lord, ex-
3. De-scend, ce - les - tial Dove! With all Thy quick'ning pow'rs; Dis-close a Sav-ior's

turn; Lord, make these mo-ments blest; From the low train of mor-tal toys, We
tend, While saints ad-dress Thy face; Let sin-ners feel Thy quick'ning word, And
love, And bless these sa - cred hours; Then shall our souls new life ob-tain, Nor

soar to reach im - mor-tal joys, We soar to reach im-mor-tal joys.
learn to know and fear the Lord, And learn to know and fear the Lord
Sab-baths be be-stowed in vain, Nor Sab - baths be be-stowed in vain.

No. 76.   Migdol.   L. M.

ISAAC WATTS.

LOWELL MASON.

1. Je-sus shall reign wher-e'er the sun Does his suc - ces - sive jour-neys run;
2. From north to south the princ-es meet, To pay their hom-age at His feet;
3. To Him shall end-less pray'r be made, And end - less prais - es crown His head;
4. Peo-ple and realms of ev - 'ry tongue Dwell on His love with sweet-est song,

His kingdom spread from shore to shore, Till moons shall wax and wane no more.
While west-ern em-pires own their Lord, And sav - age tribes at-tend His word.
His name like sweet per-fume shall rise With ev - 'ry morn-ing sac - ri - fice.
And in-fant voic-es shall pro-claim Their ear - ly bless-ings on His name.

No. 77.   Appleton.   L. M.

ISAAC WATTS.

WILLIAM BOYCE.

1. God is the ref - uge of His saints, When storms of sharp dis-tress in - vade;
2. Let mountains from their seats be hurled Down to the deep, and bur - ied there,
3. Loud may the trou-bled o-cean roar; In sa-cred peace our souls a - bide;
4. There is a stream whose gen-tle flow Sup-plies the cit - y of our God,
5. That sa-cred stream, Thine ho-ly word, Our grief al-lays, our fear con - trols;
6. Zi - on en-joys her Monarch's love, Se - cure a-gainst a threat-'ning hour;

Ere we can of - fer our com-plaints, Be-hold Him pres - ent with His aid.
Con - vul-sions shake the sol - id world,—Our faith shall nev-er yield to fear.
While ev -'ry na - tion, ev - 'ry shore, Trem-bles, and dreads the swelling tide.
Life, love and joy, still glid-ing thro' And wa-t'ring our di - vine a - bode.
Sweet peace Thy prom-is - es af - ford, And give new strength to faint-ing souls.
Nor can her firm foun-da-tion move, Built on His truth, and armed with pow'r.

No. 78. Hark! the Voice of Jesus Calling.

MARY B. SLEIGHT.   H. R. PALMER, by Per.

1. Hark! the voice of Je - sus call - ing, "Fol-low me, fol-low me!"
2. Who will heed the ho - ly man-date, "Fol-low me, fol-low me!"
3. Heark-en, lest He plead no long - er, "Fol-low me, fol-low me!"

Soft - ly thro' the si - lence fall - ing, "Fol-low, fol - low me!"
Leav - ing all things at His bid-ding, "Fol-low, fol - low me!"
Once a - gain, O, hear Him call - ing, "Fol-low, fol - low me!"

As of old He called the fish - ers, When He walked by Gal - i - lee,
Hark! that ten - der voice en - treat - ing Mar - i - ners on life's rough sea,
Turn - ing swift at Thy sweet sum-mons, Ev - er-more, O Christ, would we,

Still His pa - tient voice is plead-ing, "Fol-low, fol - low me!"
Gen - tly, lov - ing - ly re - peat - ing, "Fol-low, fol - low me!"
For Thy love all else for - sak - ing, "Fol-low, fol - low Thee!"

No. 79.   Old Hundred.   L. M.

PSALM 100   GUILLAUME FRANC.

1. All peo-ple that on earth do dwell, Sing to the Lord with cheer-ful voice,
2. Know that the Lord is God in-deed; With-out our aid He did us make:
3. O, 'en-ter then His gates with joy, With-in His courts His praise pro-claim;
4. Be-cause the Lord our God is good, His mer-cy is for-ev-er sure;

Him serve with mirth, His praise forth tell, Come ye be-fore Him and re-joice.
We are His flock, He doth us feed, And for His sheep He doth us take.
Let thank-ful songs your tongues em-ploy, O, bless and mag-ni-fy His name.
His truth at all times firm-ly stood, And shall from age to age en-dure.

No. 80.   Laban.   S. M.

GEORGE HEATH.   LOWELL MASON.

1. My soul, be on thy guard, Ten thou-sand foes a-rise,
2. O, watch, and fight, and pray, The bat-tle ne'er give o'er,
3. Ne'er think the vic-t'ry won, Nor lay thine ar-mor down;
4. Fight on, my soul, till death Shall bring Thee to Thy God:

And hosts of sin are press-ing hard To draw thee from the skies.
Re-new it bold-ly ev-'ry day, And help di-vine im-plore.
The work of faith will not be done Till thou ob-tain the crown.
He'll take thee, at thy part-ing breath, To His di-vine a-bode.

No. 81. God Be With You.

J. E. RANKIN.   W. G. TOMER.

1. God be with you till we meet a - gain, By His coun-sels guide up-
2. God be with you till we meet a - gain, 'Neath His wings pro-tect-ing,
3. God be with you till we meet a - gain, When life's per-ils thick con-
4. God be with you till we meet a - gain, Keep love's ban-ner float-ing

hold. you, With His sheep se - cure - ly fold you,
hide you, Dai - ly man - na still pro - vide you,
found you, Put His arms un - fail - ing round you,
o'er you, Smite death's threat-'ning wave be - fore you,

CHORUS.

God be with you till we meet a - gain. Till me meet, till we
                                         Till we meet, till we

meet, Till we meet at Je - sus' feet. Till we
meet, till we meet,   till we meet,

meet, till we meet, God be with you till we meet a - gain.
Till we meet, till we meet, till we meet,

Kind Words Can Never Die.

Miss A. HUTCHINSON.   ABBY HUTCHINSON.

1. Kind words can nev-er die, Cher-ished and blest, God knows how deep they lie,
2. Sweet tho'ts can nev-er die, Tho', like the flow'rs, Their bright-est hues may fly
3. Our souls can nev-er die, Tho' in the tomb We may all have to lie.

Stored in the breast; Like childhood's simple rhymes, Said o'er a thou-sand times,
In win-t'ry hours. But when the gen-tle dew Gives them their charm a-new,
Wrapped in its gloom. What tho' the flesh de-cay, Souls pass in peace a-way,

Ay, in all years and climes Dis-tant and near. Kind words can nev-er die,
With many an add-ed hue They bloom a-gain. Sweet tho'ts can nev-er die,
Live thro' e-ter-nal day With Christ a-bove. Our souls can nev-er die,

Nev-er die, nev-er die, Kind words can nev-er die, No, nev-er die.
Nev-er die, nev-er die, Sweet tho'ts can nev-er die, No, nev-er die.
Nev-er die, nev-er die, Our souls can nev-er die, No, nev-er die.

Blessed Assurance.

FANNY J. CROSBY.   Mrs. JOSEPH F. KNAPP.

1. Bless - ed as - sur - ance, Je - sus is mine, O, what a
2. Per - fect sub - mis - sion, per - fect de - light, Vis - ions of
3. Per - fect sub - mis - sion, all is at rest, I in my

fore - taste of glo - ry di - vine! Heir of sal - va - tion, pur-chase of
rap - ture now burst on my sight, An - gels de-scend - ing, bring from a-
Sav - ior am hap - py and blest, Watch-ing and wait - ing, look-ing a-

CHORUS.

God, Born of His Spir - it, washed in His blood.)
bove, Ech-oes of mer - cy, whis-pers of love. } This is my sto - ry,
bove, Filled with His good-ness, lost in His love.)

this is my song, Prais-ing my Sav - ior all the day long; This is my

sto - ry, This is my song, Prais-ing my Sav - ior all the day long.

No. 84.   Lyons.   10. 11.

SIR ROBERT GRANT.   FRANCIS JOSEPH HAYDN.

1. O, wor-ship the King all-glo-rious a-bove, And grate-ful-ly
2. O, tell of His might, and sing of His grace, Whose robe is the
3. Thy boun-ti-ful care what tongue can re-cite? It breathes in the
4. Frail chil-dren of dust, and fee-ble as frail, In Thee do we

sing His won-der-ful love; Our Shield and De-fend-er, the
light, whose can-o-py space; His char-iots of wrath the deep
air, it shines in the light, It streams from the hills, it de-
trust, nor find Thee to fail; Thy mer-cies how ten-der! how

An-cient of days, Pa-vil-ioned in splen-dor, and gird-ed with praise.
thun-der-clouds form, And dark is His path on the wings of the storm.
scends to the plain, And sweet-ly dis-tills in the dew and the rain.
firm to the end! Our Mak-er, De-fend-er, Re-deem-er and Friend.

No. 85.   Geneva.   C. M.

(SEE HYMN 10.)   JOHN COLE.

1. When all Thy mer-cies, O, my God, My ris-ing soul sur-veys,
When all Thy mercies, O my God,

When all Thy mercies, O, my God,

Geneva.

Trans-port - ed with the view, I'm lost In won - der, love, and praise.

Transported with the view, I'm lost,

No. 86. **Varina. C. M.**

ISAAC WATTS.

GEO. F. ROOT.

1. There is a land of pure de-light, Where saints immortal reign; In - fi-nite day ex-
2. Sweet fields beyond the swelling flood Stand dress'd in living green, So to the Jews old

cludes the night, And pleasures ban-ish pain. There ev-er-last-ing Spring a-bides, And
Canaan stood, While Jordan rolled between. Could we but climb where Moses stood, And

never-with'ring flow'rs: Death, like a narrow sea, divides This heav'nly land from ours.
view the landscape o'er, Not Jordan's stream, nor death's cold flood, Should fright us from the shore.

No. 87.   Amsterdam.   7, 6, 7.

ROBERT SEAGRAVE.   JAMES NARES.

1. Rise, my soul, and stretch thy wings, Thy bet-ter por-tion trace; Rise from tran-si-
2. Riv - ers to the o-cean run, Nor stay in all their course; Fire as-cend-ing
3. Cease, ye pil-grims, cease to mourn, Press on-ward to the prize; Soon our Sav-ior

to-ry things Toward heav'n, thy native place: Sun, and moon, and stars de-cay; Time shall
seeks the sun; Both speed them to their source: So a soul that's born of God, Pants to
will re-turn Tri-umph-ant in the skies: There we'll join the heav'nly train, Welcomed

soon this earth re-move; Rise, my soul, and haste a - way To seats prepared a-bove.
view His glo-rious face: Up-ward tends to His a - bode, To rest in His em-brace.
to par-take the bliss; Fly from sor-row, care, and pain, To realms of end-less peace.

No. 88.   Frederick.   11.

W. A. MUHLENBERG.   G. KINGSLEY.

1. I would not live al-way; I   ask not to stay Where storm af - ter
2. I would not live al-way; no,   wel-come the tomb; Since Je - sus hath
3. Who, who would live al-way a - way from his God, A - way from yon
4. Where saints of all a - ges in   har - mo-ny meet, Their Sav-ior and

Frederick.

storm ris - es dark o'er the way; The few lu - rid morn-ings that
lain there, "I dread not its gloom; There sweet be my rest till He
heav - en, that bliss - ful a - bode Where the riv - ers of pleas - ure flow
breth - ren trans-port - ed to greet; While the an-thems of rap - ture un-

dawn on us here Are e-nough for life's woes, full e - nough for its cheer.
bid me a - rise To hail Him in tri-umph de - scend-ing the skies.
o'er the bright plains, And the noon-tide of glo - ry e - ter - nal-ly reigns?
ceas - ing - ly roll, And the smile of the Lord is the feast of the soul.

No. 89. Stand Up for Jesus. 7, 6.

GEORGE DUFFIELD, Jr.   G. J. WEBB,

1. Stand up! stand up for Je - sus! Ye sol-diers of the cross; Lift high His
2. Stand up! stand up for Je - sus! Stand in His strength a-lone; The arm of
3. Stand up! stand up for Je - sus! The strife will not be long; This day the

roy - al ban - ner, It must not suf-fer loss: From vic-t'ry un - to vic - t'ry His
flesh will fail you; You dare not trust your own: Put on the gos-pel ar - mor, And
noise of bat - tle, The next the vic-tor's song: To Him that o - ver - com - eth, A

ar - my shall He lead, Till ev -'ry foe is van-quished, And Christ is Lord in-deed.
watch-ing un-to pray'r, Where du-ty calls or dan - ger, Be nev-er want-ing there.
crown of life shall be; He with the King of glo - ry Shall reign e - ter - nal -ly.

No. 90.

Twilight.

MARY A. LATHBURY.

WM. P. SHERWIN.

1. Day is dy - ing in the west; Heav'n is touch - ing
2. Lord of life, be - neath the dome Of the u - ni-
3. While the deep - 'ning shad - ows fall, Heart of Love, en-
4. When for - ev - er from our sight, Pass the stars— the

earth with rest; Wait and wor - ship while the night
verse, Thy home; Gath - er us, who seek Thy face,
fold - ing all, Thro' the glo - ry and the grace
day— the night, Lord of an - gels, on our eyes

Sets her ev - 'ning lamps a - light Thro' all the sky.
To the fold of Thy em-brace, For Thou art nigh.
Of the stars that veil Thy face, Our hearts as - cend.
Let e - ter - nal morn - ing rise, And shad - ows end.

CHORUS.

Ho - ly, ho - ly, ho - ly, Lord, God of Hosts! Heav'n and earth are

full of Thee! Heav'n and earth are praising Thee, O Lord most high!

No. 91.   Shall I Let Him In?

H. R. PALMER.   H. R. PALMER.
Not too fast.

1. Christ is knock-ing at my sad heart; Shall I let Him in?
2. Shall I send Him the lov-ing word; Shall I let Him in?
3. Yes, I'll o-pen this heart's proud door, Yes, I'll let Him in;

Pa-tient-ly plead-ing with my sad heart; O, shall I let Him in?
Meek-ly ac-cept-ing my gra-cious Lord; O, shall I let Him in?
Glad-ly I'll wel-come Him ev-er-more; O, yes, I'll let Him in.

Cold and proud is my heart with sin; Dark and cheer-less is all with-in;
He can in-fi-nite love im-part; He can par-don this reb-el heart;
Bless-ed Sav-ior, a-bide with me; Cares and tri-als will light-er be;

Christ is bid-ding me turn un-to Him, O, shall I let Him in?
Shall I bid Him for-ev-er de-part, Or shall I let Him in?
I am safe if I'm on-ly with Thee, O, bless-ed Lord, come in.

No. 92.   Jesus is Mine.

MRS. CATHARINE J BONAR.   T. E. PERKINS.

1. Fade, fade each earth-ly joy, Je - sus is mine! Break ev-'ry
2. Tempt not my soul a - way, Je - sus is mine! Here would I
3. Fare - well, ye dreams of night, Je - sus is mine! Lost in this
4. Fare - well, mor - tal - i - ty, Je - sus is mine! Wel - come, e-

ten - der tie, Je - sus is mine! Dark is the wil - der-ness,
ev - er stay, Je - sus is mine! Per - ish - ing things of clay,
dawn - ing bright, Je - sus is mine! All that my soul has tried
ter - ni - ty, Je - sus is mine! Wel - come, O loved and blest,

Earth has no rest-ing place, Je - sus a - lone can bless, Je - sus is mine!
Born but for one brief day, Pass from my heart a - way, Je - sus is mine!
Left but a dis-mal void; Je - sus has sat - is - fied, Je - sus is mine!
Wel-come sweet scenes of rest, Welcome, my Sav-ior's breast, Je - sus is mine!

No. 93.   Silent Night.

MICHAEL HAYDN.

1. Si - lent night! Ho - ly night! All is calm, all is bright
2. Si - lent night! Ho - ly night! Shep - herds quake at the sight!
3. Si - lent night! Ho - ly night! Son of God, love's pure light

Silent Night.

Round yon vir - gin moth-er and child! Ho - ly In-fant, so ten-der and mild,
Glo - ries stream from heav-en a-far Heav - en - ly hosts sing al - le - lu - ia,
Ra-diant beams from Thy ho-ly face, With the dawn of re-deem-ing grace,

Sleep in heav - en - ly peace, Sleep in heav - en - ly peace.
Christ, the Sav - ior is born! Christ, the Sav - ior is born!
Je - sus, Lord, at Thy birth, Je - sus, Lord, at Thy birth.

No. 94. There is a Happy Land.

HINDOO MELODY.

1. There is a hap - py land, Far, far a - way, Where saints in
2. Bright in that hap - py land, Beams ev - 'ry eye; Kept by a
3. Come to that hap - py land, Come, come a - way, Why will ye

glo - ry stand, Bright, bright as day; O, how they sweet - ly sing,
Fa-ther's hand, Love can - not die. O, then, to glo - ry run;
doubt-ing stand, Why still de - lay? O, we shall hap - py be,

Wor - thy is our Sav-ior King, Loud let His prais-es ring, Praise, praise for aye!
Be a crown and kingdom won, And bright a-bove the sun, We'll reign for aye!
When from sin and sor-row free, Lord, we shall live with Thee, Blest, blest for aye!

St. Hilda. 7, 6.

HORATIUS BONAR.

REV. H. HUSBAND.

1. I lay my sins on Je-sus, The spot-less Lamb of God;
2. I lay my wants on Je-sus, All full-ness dwells in Him;
3. I rest my soul on Je-sus, This wea-ry soul of mine;
4. I long to be like Je-sus, Meek, lov-ing, low-ly, mild;

He bears them all and frees us From the ac-curs-ed load:
He heal-eth my dis-eas-es, He doth my soul re-deem:
His right hand me em-brac-es, I on His breast re-cline:
I long to be like Je-sus, The Fa-ther's ho-ly child:

I bring my guilt to Je-sus, To wash my crim-son stains
I lay my griefs on Je-sus, My bur-dens and my cares,
I love the name of Je-sus, Im-man-uel, Christ, the Lord;
I long to be with Je-sus A-mid the heav'n-ly throng;

White in His blood most pre-cious, Till not a stain re-mains.
He from them all re-leas-es, He all my sor-rows shares.
Like fra-grance on the breez-es, His name a-broad is poured.
To sing with saints His prais-es, And learn the an-gels' song.

No. 96.   We Lay Us Down to Sleep.

R. SCHUMANN.
AIR FROM "TRÄUMEREI."

1. We   lay   us calm - ly down to   sleep,   When friend-ly night is
2. As sinks   the sun in west - ern skies,   When day   is done, and
3. Why vex   our souls with wear-ing care?   Why shun the grave, for
4. Some oth - er hand the task can   take,   If   so   it seem - eth

come, and leave To God the rest; Wheth-er   we wake to smile or weep,
twi-light dim Comes si-lent on,   So fades   the world's most lur-ing prize,
ach-ing head So cool and low? Have we   found life so pass-ing fair,
best, the task By us be - gun; No work   for which we need to wake,

Or wake no more on Time's fair shore, He know-eth best, He know - eth best.
On eyes that close in deep re-pose, Till wakes the dawn, Till wakes the dawn.
So grand to be, so sweet that we Should dread to go? Should dread to   go?
In   joy or grief, for life so brief, Be-neath the sun, Be - neath the sun.

CHORUS. Cres.   Dim.   Rit e dim.

O   Fa - ther, bless in love thy child! We lay us down to sleep.

No. 97.　　　　Parting Hymn.

JOHN ELLERTON.　　　　　　　　　　　　E. J. HOPKINS.

1. Sav - ior, a - gain to Thy dear name we raise With one ac-
2. Grant us Thy peace up - on our home-ward way; With Thee be-
3. Grant us Thy peace, Lord, thro' the com - ing night, Turn Thou for
4. Grant us Thy peace through-out our earth-ly life, Our balm in

cord our part-ing hymn of praise; We stand to bless Thee ere our wor-ship
gan, with Thee shall end the day; Guard Thou the lips from sin, the hearts from
us its dark-ness in - to light; From harm and dan - ger keep Thy chil-dren
sor - row and our stay in strife; Then, when Thy voice shall bid our con-flict

Rit.

cease, Then, low - ly kneel - ing, wait Thy word of peace.
shame, That in this house have called up - on Thy name.
free, For dark and light are both a - like to Thee.
cease, Call us, O Lord, to Thy e - ter - nal peace. A - men.

No. 98.　　　　Downs. C. M.

JOHN NEWTON.　　　　　　　　　　　　LOWELL MASON.

1. How sweet the name of Je - sus sounds In a be - liev - er's ear!
2. It makes the wound-ed spir - it whole, And calms the trou - bled breast;
3. Dear name! the rock on which I build, My shield and hid - ing - place;
4. Je - sus, my Shep-herd, Sav-ior, Friend, My Proph-et, Priest, and King,
5. I would Thy bound-less love pro-claim With ev - 'ry fleet - ing breath;

Downs.

It soothes his sor - rows, heals his wounds, And drives a - way His fear.
'Tis man-na to the hun-gry soul, And to the wea - ry, rest.
My nev - er - fail - ing treas-ure, filled With bound-less stores of grace !
My Lord, my Life, my Way, my End, Ac - cept the praise I bring!
So shall the mu - sic of Thy name Re - fresh my soul in death.

No. 99. Shining Shore.

DAVID NELSON.

GEO. F. ROOT.

1. My days are glid - ing swift-ly by, And I, a pil - grim stran-ger,
2. We'll gird our loins, my breth-ren dear, Our heav'n - ly home dis - cern - ing;
3. Should com-ing days be cold and dark, We need not cease our sing - ing;
4. Let sor-row's rud - est tem-pest blow, Each cord on earth to sev - er;

Would not de-tain them as they fly, Those hours of toil and dan - ger.
Our ab-sent Lord has sent us word, Let ev - 'ry lamp be burn - ing.
That per-fect rest naught can mo-lest, Where gold - en harps are ring - ing.
Our King says, "Come," and there's our home For-ev - er, O, for - ev - er.

REFRAIN.

For, O, we stand on Jor-dan's strand, Our friends are pass-ing o - ver;

And, just be-fore the shin-ing shore We may al-most dis - cov-er!

No. 100.   Pilot.

EDWARD HOPPER.   J. E. GOULD.

1. Je - sus, Sav - ior, pi - lot me,   O - ver life's tem-pest-uous sea;
2. As a moth - er stills her child, Thou canst hush the o-cean wild;
3. When at last I near the shore, And the fear - ful break-ers roar,

Un-known waves be-fore me roll,   Hid - ing rocks and treacherous shoal;
Bois-t'rous waves o - bey Thy will   When Thou say'st to them,"Be still!"
'Twixt me and the peace-ful rest.   Then, while lean - ing on Thy breast,

Chart and com - pass came from Thee; Je - sus, Sav - ior, pi - lot me.
Won-drous Sov -'reign of the sea, Je - sus, Sav - ior, pi - lot me.
May I hear Thee say to me, "Fear not, I will pi - lot thee."

No. 101.   America.   6, 4.

SAMUEL F. SMITH.   HENRY CAREY.

1. My coun-try, 'tis of thee, Sweet land of lib - er-ty, Of thee I sing: Land where my
2. My na-tive coun-try, thee, Land of the no-ble, free, Thy name I love; I love thy
3. Let mu-sic swell the breeze, And ring from all the trees Sweet freedom's song: Let mortal
4. Our fa-thers' God! to Thee, Au-thor of lib - er-ty, To Thee we sing: Long may our

America.

fa-thers died! Land of the pilgrims' pride' From ev-'ry mountain side Let free-dom ring!
rocks and rills, Thy woods and templed hills: My heart with rapture thrills Like that above.
tongues awake; Let all that breathe partake; Let rocks their silence break, The sound prolong.
land be bright With freedom's holy light; Protect us by Thy might, Great God, our King!

No. 102. Invitation. C. M. D.

HORATIUS BONAR.

LOUIS SPOHR.

1. I heard the voice of Je-sus say, "Come un-to me and rest;
2. I heard the voice of Je-sus say, "Be-hold, I free-ly give
3. I heard the voice of Je-sus say, "I am this dark world's Light;

Lay down, thou wea-ry one, lay down Thy head up-on my breast!"
The liv-ing wa-ter; thirst-y one, Stoop down, and drink, and live!"
Look un-to me, thy morn shall rise And all thy day be bright!"

I came to Je-sus as I was, Wea-ry, and worn, and sad;
I came to Je-sus, and I drank Of that life-giv-ing stream;
I looked to Je-sus, and I found In Him my Star, my Sun;

I found in Him a rest-ing-place, And He hath made me glad.
My thirst was quenched, my soul re-vived, And now I live in Him.
And in that light of life I'll walk, Till all my jour-ney's done.

No. 103.   O Happy Day.   L. M.

PHILIP DODDRIDGE.

1. O hap-py day, that fix'd my choice On Thee, my Sav - ior and my God!
2. O hap-py bond, that seals my vows To Him who mer - its all my love!
3. 'Tis done, the great trans-ac-tion's done; I am my Lord's, and He is mine;
4. Now rest, my long di - vid - ed heart, Fix'd on this bliss - ful cen - tre, rest;

Well may this glow - ing heart re - joice, And tell its rap - tures all a - broad.
Let cheerful an - thems fill His house, While to that sa - cred shrine I move.
He drew me, and I fol-low'd on, Charm'd to con - fess the voice di - vine.
Nor ev - er from Thy Lord de - part, With Him of ev - 'ry good possessed.

CHORUS.

Hap - py day, hap - py day, When Je - sus wash'd my sins a - way;

He taught me how to watch and pray, And live re - joic - ing ev - 'ry day.

Hap - py day, hap - py day, When Je - sus wash'd my sins a - way.

No. 104.   Portuguese Hymn. 11.

GEORGE KEITH.   UNKNOWN.

1. How firm a foun - da - tion, ye saints of the Lord, Is laid for your
2. "Fear not, I am with Thee, O, be not dis - mayed, For I am thy
3. "When thro' the deep wa - ters I call thee to go, The riv - ers of
4. "When thro' fier - y tri - als thy path-way shall lie, My grace, all - suf-
5. "E'en down to old age all my peo - ple shall prove My sov-'reign, e-
6. "The soul that on Je - sus hath leaned for re - pose, I will not, I

faith in His ex - cel - lent word! What more can He say, than to
God, I will still give thee aid; I'll strength-en thee, help thee, and
sor - row shall not o - ver - flow; For I will be with thee thy
fi - cient, shall be thy sup - ply, The flame shall not hurt thee; I
ter - nal, un - change-a - ble love; And when hoar-y hairs shall their
will not de - sert to his foes; That soul, tho' all hell should en-

you He hath said, To you, who for ref - uge to Je - sus have
cause thee to stand, Up - held by my grac - ious, om - nip - o - tent
tri - als to bless, And sanc - ti - fy to thee thy deep - est dis-
on - ly de - sign Thy dross to con - sume, and thy gold to re-
tem - ples a - dorn, Like lambs they shall still in my bo - som be
deav - or to shake, I'll nev - er, no nev - er, no nev - er for-

fled? To you, who for ref - uge to Je - sus have fled?
hand, Up - held by my grac - ious, om - nip - o - tent hand.
tress, And sanc - ti - fy to thee thy deep - est dis - tress.
fine, Thy dross to con - sume, and thy gold to re - fine.
borne, Like lambs they shall still in my bo - som be borne.
sake, I'll nev - er, no nev - er, no nev - er for - sake!"

No. 105. Elmswood. S. M. D.

CHARLES WESLEY.

ISAAC B. WOODBURY.

1. Sol-diers of Christ, a - rise, And put your ar-mor on, Strong in the strength which
2. Stand, then, in His great might, With all His strength endued; But take, to arm you
3. Leave no un-guard-ed place, No weak-ness of the soul; Take ev-'ry vir-tue,

God supplies Thro' His e - ter - nal Son; Strong in the Lord of hosts, And in His
for the fight, The pan-o - ply of God: That, hav-ing all things done, And all your
ev - 'ry grace, And for-ti - fy the whole: In - dis-sol - u - bly joined, To bat-tle

might-y pow'r, Who in the strength of Je - sus trusts Is more than con-quer-or.
conflicts passed, Ye may o'er-come thro' Christ alone, And stand en-tire at last.
all pro-ceed; But arm yourselves with all the mind That was in Christ, your Head.

No. 106. Armenia. C. M.

JOHN FAWCETT.

SYLVANUS BILLINGS POND.

1. How pre - cious is the book di - vine, By in - spi - ra - tion giv'n!
2. It sweet - ly cheers our droop-ing hearts, In this dark vale of tears;
3. This lamp, thro' all the te - dious night Of life, shall guide our way;

Armenia.

Bright as   a lamp   its   doc-trines shine, To   guide our   souls to heav'n.
Life, light,   and joy   it   still im-parts, And quells our   ris - ing   fears.
Till   we   be - hold   the   clear - er   light   Of   an   e - ter - nal   day.

No. 107.   Forever With the Lord.   S. M. D.

JAMES MONTGOMERY.   I. B. WOODBURY.

1. "For - ev - er with the Lord!" A-men,   so let it   be; Life from the dead is
2. My Fa-ther's house on high,   Home of   my soul, how near, At times, to faith's as-
3. Yet doubts still in - ter-vene,   And all   my com-fort flies; Like No-ah's dove, I

in that word, 'Tis im - mor-tal - i - ty.   Here in   the bod - y   pent,
pir - ing eye Thy gold - en gates ap-pear.   Ah! then   my spir - it   faints
flit   be-tween Rough seas and storm - y skies.   A - non   the clouds de - part,

Ab - sent from Him   I   roam,   Yet night - ly   pitch my   mov - ing   tent
To   reach the land   I   love;   The bright in - her - it - ance of   saints
The   wind and wa - ters cease,   While sweet-ly   o'er   my   glad-dened heart

A day's march nearer home; Near-er home, nearer home, A day's march near-er home.
Je - ru - sa-lem   a - bove;   Home a-bove, home a-bove, Je - ru - sa-lem   a - bove.
Ex-pands the bow of   peace: Bow of peace, bow of peace, Expands the bow of peace.

No. 108.   Lebanon. S. M. D.

HORATIUS BONAR.   JOHN ZUNDEL.

1. I was a wan-d'ring sheep, I did not love the fold; I did not love my
2. The Shepherd sought His sheep, The Father sought His child; He fol-lowed me o'er
3. No more a wan-d'ring sheep, I love to be con-trolled, I love my ten - der

Shep-herd's voice, I would not be con-trolled; I was a way-ward child, I did not
vale and hill, O'er des-erts waste and wild: He found me nigh to death, Fam-ished, and
Shep-herd's voice, I love the peace-ful fold: No more a way-ward child, I seek no

love my home, I did not love my Father's voice,—I loved a - far to roam.
faint, and lone; He bound me with the bands of love, He saved the wan-d'ring one.
more to roam; I love my heav'nly Father's voice, I love, I love His home.

No. 109.   Talmar. 8, 7.

E. E. HIGBEE.   ISAAC BAKER WOODBURY.

1. Je - sus, o'er the grave vic - to - rious, Conq'ring death and conq'ring hell,
2. Down to earth in all its dark - ness, From the Fa - ther Thou didst come;
3. By a life of love and la - bor Do-ing all the Fa-ther's will;
4. Pa-tient ev - er in well - do - ing, Mov-ing on in steps of blood,

Talmar.

Reign Thou in Thy might all - glo - rious; Heav'n and earth Thy tri - umph swell.
Seek-ing sin - ners in their blind-ness, Call-ing earth's poor ex - iles home.
Giv-ing to each sup-pliant suf - f'rer Pre-cious balm for ev - 'ry ill.
Thro' the grave to heights of glo - ry, Rec - on - cil-ing us with God.

No. 110.   Ellesdie. 8, 7. D.

HENRY F. LYTE.   ARR. FROM JOHANN C. W. A. MOZART.

1. Je - sus, I my cross have tak-en, All to leave, and fol - low Thee;
2. Let the world de-spise and leave me, They have left my Sav - ior, too;
3. Go, then, earth-ly fame and treas-ure! Come, dis - as - ter, scorn, and pain!

Nak - ed, poor, de-spised, for - sak-en, Thou, from hence, my all shalt be:
Hu-man hearts and looks de-ceive me; Thou art not, like man, un - true;
In Thy serv-ice, pain is pleas-ure, With Thy fa - vor, loss is gain.

Per - ish ev - 'ry fond am - bi - tion, All I've sought, and hoped, and known;
And, while Thou shalt smile up - on me, God of wis - dom, love and might,
I have called Thee, "Ab - ba, Fa-ther;" I have stayed my heart on Thee:

Yet how rich is my con - di - tion, God and heav'n are still my own!
Foes may hate, and friends may shun me; Show Thy face, and all is bright.
Storms may howl, and clouds may gath-er, All must work for good to me.

No. 111.   Refuge.   7.   D.

CHARLES WESLEY.   JOSEPH P. HOLBROOK.

1. Je - sus, Lov - er of my soul, Let me to Thy bo - som fly,
2. Oth - er ref - uge have I none; Hangs my help - less soul on Thee:
3. Thou, O Christ, art all I want; More than all in Thee I find;
4. Plen-teous grace with Thee is found, Grace to cov - er all my sin:

While the near - er wa-ters roll, While the tem - pest still is high!
Leave, O leave me not a - lone, Still sup - port and com-fort me:
Raise the fall - en, cheer the faint, Heal the sick, and lead the blind.
Let the heal - ing streams a-bound: Make and keep me pure with - in.

Hide me, O, my Sav - ior, hide, Till the storm of life is past;
All my trust on Thee is stayed, All my help from Thee I bring;
Just and ho - ly is Thy name, I am all un-right-eous-ness:
Thou of life the fount-ain art, Free - ly let me take of Thee:

Safe in - to the ha - ven guide, O, re - ceive my soul at last!
Cov - er my de - fense-less head With the shad - ow of Thy wing!
False and full of sin I am, Thou art full of truth and grace.
Spring Thou up with - in my heart, Rise to all e - ter - ni - ty.

No. 112. Yield Not to Temptation.

H. R. PALMER.

H. R. PALMER.

1. Yield not to temp-ta-tion, For yield-ing is sin, Each vic-t'ry will
2. Shun ev-il com-pan-ions, Bad lan-guage dis-dain, God's name hold in
3. To him that o'er-com-eth God giv-eth a crown, Thro' faith we shall

help you Some oth-er to win; Fight man-ful-ly on-ward,
rev-'rence, Nor take it in vain; Be thought-ful and ear-nest,
con-quer, Tho' oft-en cast down; He who is our Sav-ior,

Dark pas-sions sub-due, Look ev-er to Je-sus, He'll car-ry you through.
Kind-heart-ed and true, Look ev-er to Je-sus, He'll car-ry you through.
Our strength will re-new, Look ev-er to Je-sus, He'll car-ry you through.

CHORUS.

Ask the Sav-ior to help you, Com-fort, strength-en, and keep you:

He is will-ing to aid you, He will car-ry you through.

No. 113. One Sweetly Solemn Thought.

PHŒBE CARY.

PHILIP PHILLIPS.

1. One sweet - ly sol - emn thought Comes to me o'er and o'er; I'm
2. Near - er my Fa - ther's house, Where ma - ny man-sions be; Near-
3. Near - er the bound of life, Where bur - dens are laid down; Near-
4. Be near me when my feet Are slip - ping o'er the brink, For

CHORUS.

near - er home to - day, to-day, Than I have been be - fore.
er the great white throne to-day, Near-er the crys tal sea.
er to leave the cross to-day, And near-er to the crown.   } Near-er my home,
I am near-er home to-day, Per-haps, than now I think.

Near-er my home, Near-er my home to-day, to-day, Than I have been be - fore.

No. 114. Mornington. S. M.

H. HARBAUGH.

EARL OF MORNINGTON.
AD. BY LOWELL MASON.

1. Je - sus! I live to Thee, The lov - li - est and best;
2. Je - sus! I die to Thee When - ev - er death shall come:
3. Wheth - er to live or die, I know not which is best;
4. Liv - ing or dy - ing, Lord, I ask but to be Thine;

Mornington.

My life in Thee, Thy life in me, In Thy blest love I rest.
To die in Thee is life to me In my e - ter - nal home.
To live in Thee is bliss to me, To die is end - less rest.
My life in Thee, Thy life in me, Makes heav'n for - ev - er mine.

No. 115.   Love Divine. 8, 7. D.

CHARLES WESLEY.   JOHN ZUNDEL.

1. Love di - vine, all love ex - cel - ling, Joy of heav'n to earth come down!
2. Breathe, O, breathe Thy lov-ing Spir-it In - to ev - 'ry trou - bled breast!
3. Fin - ish, then, Thy new cre - a - tion; Pure and spot-less let us be;

Fix in us Thy hum - ble dwell-ing; All Thy faith - ful mer - cies crown.
Let us all in Thee in - her - it, Let us find the prom - ised rest.
Let us see Thy great sal - va - tion Per - fect - ly re-stored in Thee:

Je - sus, Thou art all com - pas - sion, Pure, un - bound-ed love Thou art;
Take a - way our bent to sin - ning; Al - pha and O - me - ga be;
Changed from glo - ry in - to glo - ry, Till in heav'n we take our place,

Vis - it us with Thy sal - va - tion; En - ter ev - 'ry trem - bling heart.
End of faith, as its be - gin - ning, Set our hearts at lib - er - ty.
Till we cast our crowns be - fore Thee, Lost in won - der, love, and praise.

No. 116.   Austria. 8, 7. D.

JOHN NEWTON.

FRANCIS JOSEPH HAYDN.

1. Glo-rious things of thee are spok-en, Zi - on, cit - y of our God;
2. See, the streams of liv - ing wa - ters, Spring-ing from e - ter - nal love,
3. Round each hab - i - ta-tion hov-'ring, See the cloud and fire ap - pear,

He, whose word can - not be brok - en, Formed thee for His own a - bode;
Still sup-ply thy sons and daugh-ters, And all fear of want re - move:
For a glo - ry and a cov-'ring, Show-ing that the Lord is near!

On the Rock of a - ges found - ed, What can shake thy sure re - pose?
Who can faint while such a riv - er Ev - er flows our thirst t' as-suage?
He who gives us dai - ly man - na, He who lis-tens when we cry,

With sal - va - tion's walls sur-round-ed, Thou may'st smile at all thy foes.
Grace, which, like the Lord, the giv - er, Nev - er fails from age to age.
Let Him hear the loud. ho - san - na Ris - ing to His throne on high.

No. 117.   To-day the Savior Calls.

S. F. SMITH, D. D.

LOWELL MASON.

1. To-day the Savior calls; Ye wand'rers, come; O, ye benighted souls, Why long-er roam?
2. To-day the Savior calls, O, hear Him now; Within these sacred walls To Je - sus bow.
3. To-day the Savior calls; For ref-uge fly; The storm of justice falls, And death is nigh.
4. The Spir-it calls to-day; Yield to His pow'r; O, grieve Him not away, 'Tis mercy's hour.

No. 118.   Cleansing Fountain.

W. COWPER.   WESTERN MELODY.

1. There is a fount-ain filled with blood, Drawn from Im - man - uel's veins;
2. The dy - ing thief re - joiced to see That fount-ain in his day;
3. Dear dy - ing Lamb, Thy pre - cious blood Shall nev - er lose its pow'r,
4. E'er since, by faith, I saw the stream Thy flow - ing wounds sup - ply,
5. Then in a no - bler, sweet - er song, I'll sing Thy pow'r to save,

And sin - ners plunged be-neath that flood, Lose all their guilt - y stains,
And there may I, tho' vile as he, Wash all my sins a - way,
Till all the ran-somed church of God Be saved to sin no more,
Re - deem - ing love has been my theme, And shall be, till I die,
When this poor lisp - ing, stam-'ring tongue, Lies si - lent in the grave,

Lose all their guilt - y stains, Lose all their guilt - y stains;
Wash all my sins a - way, Wash all my sins a - way;
Be saved to sin no more, Be saved to sin no more;
And shall be, till I die, And shall be, till I die;
Lies si - lent in the grave, Lies si - lent in the grave;

And sin-ners plunged be-neath that flood, Lose all their guilt - y stains.
And there may I, tho' vile as he, Wash all my sins a - way.
Till all the ran-somed church of God Be saved to sin no more.
Re - deem - ing love has been my theme, And shall be till I die.
When this poor lisp - ing, stam-'ring tongue, Lies si - lent in the grave.

No. 119.   Italian Hymn.

CHARLES WESLEY.   F. GIARDINI.

1. Come, Thou Al - might - y King, Help us Thy name to sing;
2. Come, Thou In - car - nate Word, Gird on Thy might - y sword,
3. Come, Ho - ly Com - fort - er, Thy sa - cred wit - ness bear,
4. To Thee, great One and Three, E - ter - nal prais - es be

Help us to praise! Fa - ther all glo - ri - ous, O'er all vic-
Our pray'r at - tend; Come and Thy peo - ple bless, And give Thy
In this glad hour: Thou who al - might - y art, Now rule in
Hence, ev - er - more: Thy sov - 'reign maj - es - ty May we in

to - ri - ous, Come and reign o - ver us, An - cient of Days.
Word suc - cess; Spir - it of ho - li - ness, On us de - scend.
ev - 'ry heart, And ne'er from us de - part, Spir - it of pow'r.
glo - ry see, And to e - ter - ni - ty, Love and a - dore!

No. 120.   Flemming.   8, 6.

CHARLOTTE ELLIOT.   F. F. FLEMMING.

1. O, ho - ly Sav - ior! Friend un - seen, Since on Thine arm Thou bidd'st me
2. What tho' the world de - ceit - ful prove, And earth-ly friends and hopes re-
3. Tho' oft I seem to tread a - lone Life's dreary waste, with thorns o'er-
4. Tho' faith and hope are oft - en tried, I ask not, need not, aught be-

Flemming.

lean, Help me, thro'out life's chang-ing scene, By faith to cling to Thee.
move; With pa-tient, un - com-plain-ing love, Still would I cling to Thee.
grown, Thy voice of love. in gent - lest tone, Still whispers, "Cling to me!"
side; So safe, so calm, so sat - is - fied, The soul that clings to Thee.

No. 121. Revive Us Again.

WM. PATON MACKAY. J. J. HUSBAND.

1. We praise Thee, O God! for the Son of Thy love, For Je - sus who
2. We praise Thee, O God! for Thy Spir - it of light, Who has shown us our
3. All glo - ry and praise to the Lamb that was slain, Who has borne all our
4. All glo - ry and praise to the God of all grace, Who has bought us, and
5. Re - vive us a - gain, fill each heart with Thy love; May each soul be re-

CHORUS.

died, and is now gone a - bove.
Sav - ior and scat-tered our night.
sins, and has cleansed ev-'ry stain. } Hal - le - lu-jah! Thine the glo - ry; Hal - le-
sought us, and guid - ed our ways.
kin-dled with fire from a - bove.

lu -jah! A - men! Hal-le - lu-jah! Thine the glo - ry; Re - vive us a - gain.

No. 122.   Ewing.   7. 6.

BERNARD OF CLUNY.
TR. BY J. M. NEALE.

ALEXANDER EWING.

1. Je - ru - sa - lem the gold - en, With milk and hon-ey blest, Be-neath thy con-tem-
2. They stand, those halls of Zi - on, All   ju-bi-lant with song, And bright with many an
3. There is the throne of   Da-vid; And there, from care released, The song of them that
4. O, sweet and bless-ed coun-try, The home of God's e - lect!   O, sweet and bless-ed

pla - tion Sink heart and voice op-prest: I know not, O, I   know   not What
an - gel, And   all the mar-tyr throng: The Prince is   ev - er   in   them. The
tri - umph, The shout of them that feast; And they who, with their Lead - er, Have
coun - try That   ea - ger hearts ex-pect!   Je - sus, in   mer-cy bring   us To

joys a-wait us there; What ra-dian - cy of glo - ry, What light beyond compare.
day-light is se-rene; The past-ures of the bless - ed Are decked in glorious sheen.
con-quered in the fight, For - ev - er and for - ev - er Are clad in robes of white.
that dear land of rest; Who art, with God the   Fa-ther, And Spir-it, ev - er blest.

No. 123.   Gloria Patri.

CHARLES MEINEKE.

Glo - ry be to the Fa - ther, and to the Son, and to the Ho - ly Ghost, as it

Gloria Patri.

was in the be-gin-ning, is now and ev-er shall be, world without end. A-men, A-men.

No. 124.   **Harwell.**   **8, 7.**   **D.**

T. KELLY.

LOWELL MASON.

1. Hark! ten thou-sand harps and voic - es Sound the notes of praise a - bove;
2. Je - sus, hail, whose glo - ry bright-ens All a - bove, and gives it worth;
3. King of glo - ry, reign for - ev - er, Thine an ev - er - last - ing crown;
4. Sav - ior, has - ten Thine ap-pear - ing, Bring, O, bring the glo-rious day;

Je - sus reigns and heav'n re - joic - es, Je - sus reigns, the God of love.
Lord of life, Thy smile en-light-ens, Cheers and charms Thy saints on earth,
Noth-ing from Thy love shall sev - er Those whom Thou hast made Thine own.
When the aw - ful sum-mons hear-ing, Heav'n and earth shall pass a - way;

See, He sits on yon-der throne, Je - sus rules the world a - lone.
When we think of love like Thine, Lord, we own it love di - vine.
Hap - py ob - ject of Thy grace, Chos - en to be-hold Thy face.
Then with gold-en harps we'll sing, "Glo - ry, glo - ry to our King."

Hal - le - lu - jah, hal - le - lu - jah, Hal - le - lu - jah, A - men.

No. 125.   Still, Still With Thee.

HARRIET BEECHER STOWE.   MENDELSSOHN.

1. Still, still with Thee, when pur-ple morn-ing break - eth, When the bird
2. A - lone with Thee, a - mid the mys - tic shad - ows, The sol - emn
3. When sinks the soul, sub-dued by toil, to slum - ber, Its clos - ing
4. So shall it be at last, in that bright morn - ing, When the soul

wak - eth, and the shad-ows flee; Fair - er than morn - ing, lov - li - er than
hush of na-ture new - ly born; A - lone with Thee in breath-less ad - o-
eye looks up to Thee in pray'r; Sweet the re - pose be-neath Thy wings o'er-
wak - eth, and life's shad-ows flee; O, in that hour, fair - er than day-light

day - light, Dawns the sweet con - scious-ness, I am with Thee.
ra - tion, In the calm dew and fresh-ness of the morn.
shad - ing, But sweet - er still, to wake and find Thee there.
dawn - ing, Shall rise the glo - rious tho't—I am with Thee.   A - men.

No. 126.   Meribah.   C. P. M.

PSALM 31 : 16-19.   LOWELL MASON.
Moderato.

1. How great the good-ness Thou hast stored In   se - cret for Thy saints, O Lord,
2. Thou in the se-cret of Thy face, Shalt find for them a hid - ing place,
3. O, let Je - ho-vah bless-ed be, Who showed His wondrous love to me
4. O, love the Lord all that Him serve, For He the faith-ful shall pre-serve,

Meribah.

Thy ho - ly name who fear! How great the mer-cies wrought for those
From proud op-press - or's wrongs; A safe re - treat for them pre-pare,
In cit - y for - ti - fied; "Cut off from Thee," I said in fear,
And all the proud re - ward. Be of good cour - age; He with strength

Who do in Thee their trust re - pose, Be - fore men's sons ap - pear.
And keep them in a cov - ert there, Se - cure from strife of tongues.
Yet Thou my sup-pliant voice didst hear, When un - to Thee I cried.
Will fill your stead-fast hearts at length, All ye who trust the Lord.

No. 127.   Mendebras. 7, 6. D.

C. WORDSWORTH.

1. O day of rest and glad-ness, O day of joy and light, O balm of care and
2. To - day on wea - ry na-tions The heav'n-ly man-na falls; To ho - ly con-vo-
3. New grac - es ev - er gain-ing From this our day of rest, We reach the rest re-

sad - ness, Most beau-ti - ful, most bright; On thee, the high and low - ly, Thro'
ca - tions The sil - ver trum-pet calls, Where gos - pel light is glow-ing With
main-ing To spir - its of the blest; To Ho - ly Ghost be prais - es, To

a - ges joined in tune, Sing "Ho-ly, ho - ly, ho - ly," To the great God Tri-une.
pure and ra-diant beams, And liv-ing wa - ters flow-ing With soul-re-fresh-ing streams.
Fa-ther, and to Son; The Church her voice up-rais-es To Thee, blest Three in One.

No. 128.   Galilee.

ROBERT MORRIS, LL. D.   H. R. PALMER.

1. Each coo - ing dove   and sigh - ing bough,   That makes the
2. Each flow - 'ry glen   and moss - y dell,   Where hap - py
3. And when I read   the thrill-ing lore   Of Him who
   Each coo-ing dove   and sigh-ing bough,

eve   so blest to me,   Has some-thing far   di-vin - er
birds   in song a - gree,   Thro' sun-ny morn   the prais-es
walked   up-on the sea,   I long, O, how   I long once
That makes the eve so blest to me,   Has something far

now,   It bears me back   to Gal - i - lee.
tell   Of sights and sounds   in Gal - i - lee.
more   To fol - low Him   in Gal - i - lee.
   di-vin - er now,   It bears me back   to Gal - i - lee.

Chorus.

O Gal - i - lee! sweet Gal - i - lee! Where Je - sus loved so much to be; O

Gal - i - lee! blue Gal - i - lee! Come, sing thy song a - gain to me!

No. 129.   Fortress.

"EIN FESTE BURG."   MARTIN LUTHER.

1. A might - y Fort-ress is   our God, A trust - y Shield and Weap - on;
2. With might of ours can naught be done, Soon were our loss ef - fect - ed;
3. Tho' dev - ils all   the world should fill, All watch-ing to   de - vour   us,
4. The Word they still shall let   re-main, And nev - er thanks have for   it,

He helps us   free from ev - 'ry need That hath us now o'er - tak - en.
But for   us fights the Val - iant One Whom God Him-self e - lect - ed.
We trem-ble not, we fear no ill, They can-not o - ver - pow'r us.
He's by our   side up - on   the plain, With His good gifts and Spir - it.

The old   bit - ter foe Means us   dead-ly woe: Deep guile and great might
Ask ye,   Who is this? Je - sus Christ it   is, The Lord Sa - ba - oth,
This world's prince may still Scowl fierce as he will, he can harm us   none,
Take they   then our life, Goods, fame, child and wife; When their worst is done,

Are his dread arms in fight, On   earth is not his e - qual.
And there's none oth - er God, He holds the field for - ev - er.
He's judged, the deed is done, One lit - tle word o'er - throws   him.
They yet have noth - ing won, The King-dom ours re - main - eth.

No. 130.   Lux Benigna.   10, 4, 10.

JOHN H. NEWMAN.   Rev. JOHN BACCHUS DYKES.

1. Lead, kind-ly Light, amid th'en-cir-cling gloom, Lead Thou me on! The night is
2. I was not ev-er thus, nor prayed that Thou Shouldst lead me on; I loved to
3. So long Thy pow'r hath blest me, sure it still Will lead me on O'er moor and

dark, and I am far from home; Lead Thou me on! Keep Thou my feet; I
choose and see my path; but now Lead Thou me on! I loved the gar - ish
fen, o'er crag and tor-rent, till The night is gone, And with the morn those

do not ask to see The dis - tant scene; one step e-nough for me.
day, and, spite of fears, Pride ruled my will. Re-mem-ber not past years!
an-gel fa - ces smile Which I have loved long since, and lost a - while.

No. 131.   Ozrem.   S. M.

CHARLES WESLEY.   ISAAC BAKER WOODBURY.

1. Lord, if at Thy com - mand The word of life we sow,
2. The vir - tue of Thy grace A large in - crease shall give,
3. Now, then, the cease - less show'r Of gos - pel bless - ings send,
4. On mul - ti - tudes con - fer The heart - re - new - ing love,

Ozrem.

Wa-tered	by	Thy al-might-y hand,	The seed shall	sure - ly grow.
And	mul - ti -	ply the faith-ful race	Who to Thy	glo - ry live.
And	let the	soul-con-vert-ing pow'r	Thy min - is -	ters at - tend.
And	by the	joy of grace pre-pare	For full - er	joys a - bove.

No. 132. Tersanctus.

UNKNOWN.

Therefore with angels and archangels, and with all the company of.... } heav'n. { We laud and magnify Thy glorious.......... } name,

Ev - er-more prais - ing Thee, and say - ing, Ho - ly, Ho - ly,

Crescendo.

f

Ho - ly Lord God of Hosts; Heav'n and earth are full of.... Thy

p *Cres.* *f*

glo - ry: Glo - ry be to Thee, O Lord, Most High. A - men.

No. 133. Nearing the Shore.

E. O. LYTE.   E. O. LYTE.

Moderato.

1. We are near - ing the heav - en - ly shore, Hap - py home of the
2. Tho' the bil - lows a-round us may roll, And the winds dash our
3. In the har - bor we'll an - chor at last, And we'll greet all our

pure and the blest; And our sor - rows will soon all be o'er, And our
bark to and fro, Ev - 'ry wave brings us near - er our goal, Ev - 'ry
friends gone be - fore; Ev - 'ry dan - ger then hap - pi - ly past, We will

CHORUS.

la - bors be turned in - to rest. ⎱
wind t'ward the place we would go. ⎰ We are near - ing, We are
rest on the heav - en - ly shore. ⎰

near-ing the shore,

near - ing, We are near - ing the heav-en - ly shore; We are
near-ing the shore,   heav-en - ly shore;

near - ing, We are near - ing, We are near-ing the heav-en-ly shore.

No. 134. Creation. L. M. D.

JOSEPH ADDISON. HAYDN.

1. The spa - cious fir - ma - ment on high, With all the blue e-
2. Soon as the ev - 'ning shades pre - vail The moon takes up the
3. What tho' in sol - emn si - lence all Move round the dark ter-

the - real sky, And span-gled heav'ns, a shin - ing frame, Their
won - drous tale, And night - ly to the list - 'ning earth Re-
res - trial ball? What tho' no re - al voice nor sound A-

great O - rig - i - nal pro-claim. Th'un-wea-ried sun, from day to day,
peats the sto - ry of her birth; While all the stars that round her burn,
mid. the ra - diant orbs be found? In rea - son's ear they all re - joice,

Does his Cre - a - tor's pow'rs dis-play, And pub - lish - es to
And all the plan - ets in their turn, Con - firm the tid - ings
And ut - ter forth a glo - rious voice, For - ev - er sing - ing

ev - 'ry land The work of an al - might - y hand.
as they roll, And spread the truth from pole to pole.
as they shine, "The hand that made us is di - vine."

No. 135.   Mendon.   L. M.

UNKNOWN.   GERMAN MELODY.

1. Great God of na - tions, now to Thee,   Our hymn of grat - i - tude we raise;
2. Thy name we bless, Al-might - y God,   For all the kind-uess Thou hast shown
3. Here free-dom spreads her ban - ner wide,   And casts her soft and hal-lowed ray;
4. We praise Thee that the gos - pel's light Thro' all our land its ra-diance sheds;
5. Great God, pre-serve us in Thy fear;   In dan - ger still our Guardian be;

With hum-ble heart, and bend - ing knee, We of - fer Thee our song of praise.
To this fair land the pil-grims trod,—This land we fond - ly call our own.
Here Thou our fa - thers' steps didst guide In safe - ty thro' their dan.g'rous way.
Dis-pels the shades of er - ror's night, And heav'n-ly blessings round us spreads.
O, spread Thy truth's bright precepts here; Let all the peo - ple wor - ship Thee.

No. 136.   Milwaukee.   8, 7.

WM. A. MUHLENBERG.   JOHN ZUNDEL.

1. Sav - ior, who Thy flock art feed-ing With the Shep-herd's kind-est care,
2. Now, these lit - tle ones re - ceiv-ing, Fold them in Thy gra-cious arm,
3. Nev - er, from Thy past - ure rov-ing, Let them be the li - on's prey;
4. Then, with-in Thy fold e - ter - nal, Let them find a rest - ing-place,

All the fee - ble, gent - ly lead-ing, While the lambs Thy bo - som share;
There, we know, Thy word be - liev-ing, On - ly there, se - cure from harm.
Let Thy ten - der - ness, so lov-ing, Keep them thro' life's dan-g'rous way.
Feed in past-ures ev - er ver-nal, Drink the riv - ers of Thy grace.

No. 137.   Dundee.   C. M.

ISAAC WATTS.   G. FRANC.

1. A - las! and did my Sav - ior bleed, And did my Sov-'reign die?
2. Was it for crimes that I have done, He groaned up - on the tree?
3. Well might the sun in dark-ness hide, And shut his glo - ries in,
4. Thus might I hide my blush-ing face While His dear cross ap - pears;
5. But drops of grief can ne'er re - pay The debt of love I owe;

Would He de - vote that sa - cred head For such a worm as I?
A - maz - ing pit - y! grace un-known! And love be-yond de - gree!
When Christ, the might - y Mak - er, died For man, the crea-ture's sin.
Dis - solve my heart in thank-ful - ness, And melt mine eyes to tears.
Here, Lord, I give my - self a - way,—'Tis all that I can do.

No. 138.   Awake, My Soul!   C. M.

PHILIP DODDRIDGE.   GEORGE FREDERICK HANDEL.

1. A-wake, my soul, stretch ev-'ry nerve, And press with vig-or on; A heav'n-ly
2. A cloud of wit-ness - es a-round Hold Thee in full sur - vey; For - get the
3. 'Tis God's all-an - i - mat-ing voice That calls thee from on high; 'Tis His own
4. Blest Sav-ior, in - tro-duced by Thee, Have I my race be-gun; And, crowned with

race de-mands thy zeal, And an im-mor-tal crown, And an im-mor-tal crown,
steps al-read - y trod, And on-ward urge thy way, And on-ward urge thy way.
hand pre-sents the prize To thine as - pir-ing eye, To thine as - pir-ing eye.
vic-t'ry, at Thy feet I'll lay my hon-ors down, I'll lay my hon-ors down.

No. 139.   Angel Voices, Ever Singing.

FRANCIS POTT.

SIR A. SULLIVAN.

1. An - gel voic - es, ev - er sing - ing, Round Thy throne of light,
2. Thou, who art be - yond the farth - est Mor - tal eye can scan,
3. Here, Great God, to - day we of - fer Of Thine own to Thee;

An - gel harps, for - ev - er ring - ing, Rest not day nor night;
Can it be that Thou re - gard - est Songs of sin - ful man?
And for Thine ac - cept - ance prof - fer, All un - wor - thi - ly,

Thou-sands on - ly live to bless Thee, And con - fess Thee Lord of might!
Can we feel that Thou art near us, And wilt hear us? Yea, we can!
Hearts and minds, and hands and voic - es, In our choic - est mel - o - dy.

No. 140.   Art Thou Weary?

REV. JOHN M. NEALE, D. D., TR.

W. H. MONK.

1. Art thou wea - ry, art thou lan - guid, Art thou sore distressed? "Come to me," saith
2. Hath He marks to lead me to Him, If He be my Guide?—"In His feet and
3. Is there di - a - dem, as monarch, That His brow a -dorns?—"Yea, a crown, in
4. If I find Him, if I fol - low, What His guerdon here? "Ma - ny a sor-row,

One, "and coming, Be at rest."
hands are wound-prints, And His side."
ver - y sure-ty But of thorns."
ma - ny a la - bor, Ma - ny a tear."

5 If I still hold closely to Him,
    What hath He at last?
"Sorrow vanquished, labor ended,
    Jordan passed."

6 If I ask Him to receive me,
    Will He say me nay?—
"Not till earth, and not till heaven
    Pass away."

No. 141.   Vox Angelica.

F. W. FABER.   JOHN B. DYKES.

1. Hark! hark, my soul! an - gel - ic songs are swell - ing O'er earth's green fields,
2. On - ward we go, for still we hear them sing - ing, "Come, wea - ry souls,
3. Far, far a - way, like bells at ev - 'ning peal - ing, The voice of Je -
4. Rest comes at length, tho' life be long and drear - y, The day must dawn,

and ocean's wave-beat shore; How sweet the truth those bless- ed strains are
for Je - sus bids you come;" And, thro' the dark, its ech- oes sweet-ly
sus sounds o'er land and sea; And la - den souls by thousands meekly
and darksome night be past; Faith's jour-ney ends in welcome to the

tell - ing Of that new life when sin shall be no more.
ring - ing, The mu - sic of the Gos - pel leads us home.
steal - ing, Kind Shep-herd, turn their wea - ry steps to Thee.
wea - ry, And heav'n, the heart's true home, will come at last.

p CHORUS.   *Cres.*   *f*

An - gels of Je - sus, an - gels of light, Sing - ing to

Vox Angelica.

wel - come the pil-grims of the night, Sing - ing to wel - come the

pil-grims, the pil-grims of the night. A - men, A - men.

No. 142. Siloam.

R. HEBER.

I. B. WOODBURY.

1. By cool Si - lo - am's shad - y rill How fair the lil - y grows!
2. Lo! such the child whose ear - ly feet The paths of peace have trod,
3. By cool Si - lo - am's shad - y rill The lil - y must de - cay;
4. And soon, too soon, the win - try hour Of man's ma - tur - er age
5. O thou whose in - fant feet were found With-in thy Fa - ther's shrine,
6. De - pend - ent on Thy boun-teous breath, We seek Thy grace a - lone

How sweet the breath be - neath the hill Of Shar - on's dew - y rose!
Whose se - cret heart, with influence sweet, Is up - ward drawn to God.
The rose that blooms be - neath the hill Must short - ly fade a - way.
May shake the soul with sor - row's pow'r And storm - y pas-sion's rage.
Whose years, with change-less vir - tue crowned, Were all a - like di - vine.
In childhood, man - hood and in death To keep us still Thine own.

No. 143.   The Rose of Sharon.*

WORDS AND MUSIC BY H. R. PALMER.

1. There's a Rose that is blooming for you, friend, There's a Rose that is blooming for me ;
2. Long a - go in the val-ley so fair, friend, Far a - way by the beau-ti-ful sea,
3. All in vain did they crush this fair flow'r, friend, All in vain did they shat-ter the tree,

Its perfume is pervading the world, friend, Its perfume is for you and for me.
This pure Rose in its beauty first bloom'd, friend, And it blooms still for you and for me.
For its roots, deeply bedded, sprang forth, friend, And it blooms still for you and for me.

REFRAIN

There's a Rose,...... a love-ly Rose,...... And its beauty all the world shall see;
Rose that blooms for me,   A Rose that blooms for you,

There's a Rose,...... a love-ly Rose,........ Its per-fume is for you and for me.
Rose that blooms for me,   A Rose that blooms for you,

*Of the many names given to our Savior, "The Rose of Sharon" is the most beautiful. This little hymn was written on the shores of the Mediterranean, amid the fragrance of ever-blooming roses, and beneath the match-less beauty of Italian skies. Thoughts of the Holy Land on the farther shore, and of the purity and loveliness of the life of our Savior mingled unconsciously with the surrounding beauty, and took form in this little poem and melody.

No. 144.   Just for To-day.

E. R. WILBERFORCE.   H. R. PALMER.

1. Lord, for to-mor-row and its needs I do not pray; Keep me, my God, from
2. Let me no wrong or i - dle word Un-think-ing say; Set Thou a seal up-
3. And if, to-day this life of mine Should ebb a - way, Give me Thy Sac - ra-

stain of sin, Just for to - day. Help me to la - bor ear - nest-ly,
on my lips Thro' all to - day. Let me in sea-son, Lord, be grave,
ment Di-vine, Fa - ther, to - day. So for to - mor-row and its needs

And du - ly pray; Let me be kind in word and deed, Fa - ther, to-day.
In sea-son gay; Let me be faithful to Thy grace, Dear Lord, to-day.
I do not pray; Still keep me, guide me, love me, Lord, thro' each to-day.

No. 145.   The Homeland! The Homeland!

Rev. H. R. HAWEIS.   A S. SULLIVAN.

1. The Home - land! the Home - land! The land of the free-born;
2. My Lord is in the Home - land, With an - gels bright and fair;
3. For those I love in the Home - land Are call - ing me a - way

There's no night in the Home-land, But aye the fade-less morn.
There's no sin in the Home-land, And no temp - ta - tion there.
To the rest and peace of the Home-land, And the life be - yond de - cay;

The Homeland! The Homeland!

I'm sigh - ing for the Home- land, My heart is ach - ing here;
The mu - sic of the Home- land Is ring - ing in my ears,
For there's no death in the Home- land, There's no sor - row a - bove.

There's no pain in the Home-land To which I'm draw - ing near.
And when I think of the Home-land, My eyes gush out with tears.
Christ, bring us all to the Home-land Of His e - ter - nal love. . A-men.

No. 146.   Stockwell. 8, 7.

CHRISTOPHER C. COX.   DARIUS E. JONES.

1. Si - lent - ly the shades of eve - ning Gath-er round my low - ly door;
2. Oh, the lost, the un - for - got - ten, Tho' the world be oft for - got;
3. Liv - ing in the si - lent hours, Where our spir - its on - ly blend,
4. How such ho - ly mem'ries clus - ter Like the stars when storms are past,

Si - lent - ly they bring be - fore me Fac - es I shall see no more.
Oh, the shroud-ed and the lone - ly, In our hearts they per - ish not.
They, un - link'd with earth - ly trou - ble, We still hop - ing for its end.
Point - ing up to that fair heav - en We may hope to gain at last.

No. 147. I'll Go Where You Want Me to Go.

MARY BROWN.
Andante.
CARRIE E. ROUNSEFELL.

1. It may not be on the mountain height, Or o - ver the storm - y sea;
2. Per - haps to - day there are lov - ing words Which Je - sus would have me speak—
3. There's sure - ly somewhere a low - ly place, In earth's har-vest fields so wide—

It may not be at the bat - tle's front My Lord will have need of me;
There may be now in the paths of sin Some wand'rer whom I should seek—
Where I may la - bor thro' life's short day For Je - sus the cru - ci - fied—

But if, by a still, small voice He calls To paths that I do not know,
O Sav - ior, if Thou wilt be my guide, Tho' dark and rugged the way,
So trust - ing my all to Thy ten - der care, And know - ing Thou lov - est me,

FINE.

I'll answer, dear Lord, with my hand in Thine, I'll go where you want me to go.
My voice shall ech - o the message sweet, I'll say what you want me to say.
I'll do Thy will with a heart sin - cere, I'll be what you want me to be.

D.S.—*I'll say what you want me to say, dear Lord, I'll be what you want me to be.*

REFRAIN.

D. S.

I'll go where you want me to go, dear Lord, Over mountain, or plain, or sea;

Copyright, 1894, by C. E .Rounsefell. By per.

No. 148.   St. Catherine.

FREDERICK W. FABER.   AD. BY J. G. WALTON.

1. Faith of our fa - thers! liv - ing still   In spite of dun-geon, fire, and sword:
2. Our fa-thers, chained in pris - ons dark, Were still in heart and con-science free:
3. Faith of our fa - thers! we   will love Both friend and foe in all   our strife:

Oh, how our hearts beat high with joy When-e'er we hear that glo-rious word:
How sweet would be their chil-dren's fate,   If they, like them, could die for thee!
And preach thee, too, as   love knows how, By kind-ly words and vir-tuous life:

Faith of our fa-thers! ho - ly faith! We will be true to thee   till death!

Recessional.

1 God of our fathers, known of old;
  Lord of our far-flung battle line ;
  Beneath whose awful hand we hold
  Dominion over palm and pine ;
  Lord God of Hosts, be with us yet,
  Lest we forget, lest we forget!

2 The tumult and the shouting dies;
  The captains and the kings depart;
  Still stands Thine ancient sacrifice,
  An humble and a contrite heart.
  Lord God of Hosts, be with us yet,
  Lest we forget, lest we forget!

3 Far-called our navies melt away;
  On dune and headland sinks the fire;
  Lo, all our pomp of yesterday
  Is one with Nineveh and Tyre!
  Judge of the nations, spare us yet,
  Lest we forget, lest we forget!

4 If, drunk with sight of power, we loose
  Wild tongues that have not Thee in awe;
  Such boastings as the gentiles use,
  Or lesser breeds without the law;
  Lord God of Hosts, be with us yet,
  Lest we forget, lest we forget!
                    RUDYARD KIPLING.

No. 149. Capello. S. M.

ABRAHAM H. C. MALAN.
TR. BY G. W. BETHUNE.

LOWELL MASON.

1. It is not death to die,— To leave this wea - ry road,
2. It is not death to close The eye long dimmed by tears,
3. It is not death to bear The wrench that sets us free
4. It is not death to fling A - side this sin - ful dust,
5. Je - sus, Thou Prince of life, Thy chos - en can - not die!

And, 'mid the broth - er - hood on high, To be at home with God.
And wake, in glo - ri - ous re - pose To spend e - ter - nal years.
From dun-geon chain, to breathe the air Of bound-less lib - er - ty.
And rise, on strong ex - ult - ing wing, To live a - mong the just.
Like Thee, they con-quer in the strife, To reign with Thee on high.

No. 150. Crossing the Bar.

ALFRED TENNYSON, ARR.

GEO. F. ROOT.

1. Sun - set and Ev - 'ning Star, And one clear call for me;
2. But mov - ing tide a - sleep, Too full for sound and foam,
3. Twi - light and Ev - 'ning Bell, And aft - er that the dark;
4. For tho' from time and place, The flood may bear me far,

And may there be no moan - ing bar When I put out to sea.
When that which drew from out the deep Turns a - gain to its home.
And may there be no sad fare - well, When I at last em - bark.
I hope to see my Pi - lot's face, When I have crossed the bar.

Used by per.

No. 151. Lord, With Glowing Heart I'd Praise Thee.

FLOTOW.

1. Lord, with glowing heart I'd praise Thee For the bliss Thy love bestows, For the
2. Praise, my soul, the God that sought thee, Wretched wand'rer, far a-stray, Found thee
3. Lord, this bo-som's ar-dent feel-ing Vain-ly would my lips ex-press, Low be-

pardoning grace that saves me, And the peace that from it flows: Help, O God, my
lost, and kindly brought thee From the paths of death a-way; Praise, with love's de-
fore Thy foot-stool kneeling, Deign Thy suppliant's pray'r to bless; Let Thy grace, my

weak en-deav-or; This dull soul to rap-ture raise: Thou must light the flame, or
vout-est feel-ing, Him who saw thy guilt-born fear; And the light of hope re-
soul's chief treasure, Love's pure flame within me raise; And since words can nev-er

nev-er Can my love be warmed to praise, Can my love be warmed to praise.
veal-ing, Bade the blood-stained Cross appear, Bade the blood-stained Cross appear.
measure, Let my life show forth Thy praise, Let my life show forth Thy praise.

No. 152. Too Late.

ALFRED TENNYSON.   LINDSAY, ARR. BY JOSEPH P. HOLBROOK.
SOLO (Soprano) OR DUET. VS. 1, 2, 3.

1. Late, late, so late! and dark the night, and chill! Late, late, so late! But we can enter still.
2. No light had we;—for that we do repent, And learning this, the Bridegroom will relent.
3. No light! so late! and dark and chill the night—O let us in, that we may find the light.

SOLO. (Bass.)   QUARTET.   Ending for 2d Verse. QUARTET.

"Too late, too late! ye cannot enter now." "Too late, too late! ye cannot enter now."

Fourth Verse.

4. Have we not heard the Bridegroom is   so sweet!   O   let us in, though

late, to kiss His feet;   O let us in,   O let us in, though late, to

SOLO. Bass or Contralto.   pp QUARTET.

kiss His feet. "No!   no!   too   late! ye cannot enter now!"

Responsive Readings.

No. 1. Ten Commandments.

Exodus 20, 1-17.

And God spake all these words, saying,

I. Thou shalt have no other Gods before me.

II. Thou shalt not make unto thee any graven image, or any likeness of any thing that is in heaven above, or that is in the earth beneath, or that is in the water under the earth: thou shalt not bow down thyself to them, nor serve them: for I the Lord thy God am a jealous God, visiting the iniquity of the fathers upon the children unto the third and fourth generation of them that hate me; and showing mercy unto thousands of them that love me, and keep my commandments.

III. Thou shalt not take the name of the Lord thy God in vain: for the Lord will not hold him guiltless that taketh His name in vain.

IV. Remember the Sabbath-day, to keep it holy. Six days shalt thou labor, and do all thy work: but the seventh day is the Sabbath of the Lord thy God: in it thou shalt not do any work, thou, nor thy son, nor thy daughter, thy man-servant, nor thy maid-servant, nor thy cattle, nor thy stranger that is within thy gates: for in six days the Lord made heaven and earth, the sea, and all that in them is, and rested the seventh day: wherefore the Lord blessed the Sabbath-day, and hallowed it.

V. Honor thy father and thy mother: that thy days may be long upon the land which the Lord thy God giveth thee.

VI. Thou shalt not kill.

VII. Thou shalt not commit adultery.

VIII. Thou shalt not steal.

IX. Thou shalt not bear false witness against thy neighbor.

X. Thou shalt not covet thy neighbor's house, thou shalt not covet thy neighbor's wife, nor his man-servant, nor his maid-servant, nor his ox, nor his ass, nor any thing that is thy neighbor's.

No. 2.   Wisdom.

Job 28, 12-28.

12 But where shall wisdom be found? and where is the place of understanding?

13 Man knoweth not the price thereof; neither is it found in the land of the living.

14 The depth saith, It is not in me: and the sea saith, It is not with me.

15 It cannot be gotten for gold, neither shall silver be weighed for the price thereof.

16 It cannot be valued with the gold of Ophir, with the precious onyx, or the sapphire.

17 The gold and the crystal cannot equal it: and the exchange of it shall not be for jewels of fine gold.

18 No mention shall be made of coral, or of pearls: for the price of wisdom is above rubies.

19 The topaz of Ethiopia shall not equal it, neither shall it be valued with pure gold.

20 Whence then cometh wisdom? and where is the place of understanding?

21 Seeing it is hid from the eyes of all living, and kept close from the fowls of the air.

22 Destruction and death say, We have heard the fame thereof with our ears.

23 God understandeth the way thereof, and He knoweth the place thereof.

24 For He looketh to the ends of the earth, and seeth under the whole heaven;

25 To make the weight for the winds; and He weigheth the waters by measure.

26 When He made a decree for the rain, and a way for the lightning of the thunder:

27 Then did He see it, and declare it; He prepared it, yea, and searched it out.

28 And unto man He said, Behold, the fear of the Lord, that is wisdom; and to depart from evil is understanding.

No. 3.   Psalm 1.

1 Blessed is the man that walketh not in the counsel of the ungodly, nor standeth in the way of sinners, nor sitteth in the seat of the scornful.

2 But his delight is in the law of the Lord; and in His law doth he meditate day and night.

3 And he shall be like a tree planted by the rivers of water, that bringeth forth his fruit in his season; his leaf also shall not wither; and whatsoever he doeth shall prosper.

4 The ungodly are not so: but are like the chaff which the wind driveth away.

5 Therefore the ungodly shall not stand in the judgment, nor sinners in the congregation of the righteous.

6 For the Lord knoweth the way of the righteous: but the way of the ungodly shall perish.

No. 4.   Psalm 8.

1 O Lord our Lord, how excellent is Thy name in all the earth! who hast set Thy glory above the heavens. •

2 Out of the mouth of babes and sucklings hast Thou ordained strength because of Thine enemies, that Thou mightest still the enemy and the avenger.

3 When I consider Thy heavens, the work of Thy fingers, the moon and the stars, which Thou hast ordained;

4 What is man, that Thou art mindful of him? and the son of man, that Thou visitest him?

5 For Thou hast made him a little lower than the angels, and hast crowned him with glory and honor.

6 Thou madest him to have dominion over the works of Thy hands; Thou hast put all things under his feet:

7 All sheep and oxen, yea, and the beasts of the field;

8 The fowl of the air, and the fish of the sea, and whatsoever passeth through the paths of the seas.

9 O Lord our Lord, how excellent is Thy name in all the earth!

No. 5.   Psalm 15.

1 Lord, who shall abide in Thy tabernacle? who shall dwell in Thy holy hill?

2 He that walketh uprightly, and worketh righteousness, and speaketh the truth in his heart.

3 He that backbiteth not with his tongue, nor doeth evil to his neighbor, nor taketh up a reproach against his neighbor.

4 In whose eyes a vile person is contemned; but He honoreth them that fear the Lord. He that sweareth to his own hurt, and changeth not.

5 He that putteth not out his money to usury, nor taketh reward against the innocent. He that doeth these things shall never be moved.

No. 6.   Psalm 19.

1 The heavens declare the glory of God; and the firmament showeth his handywork.

2 Day unto day uttereth speech, and night unto night showeth knowledge.

3 There is no speech nor language, where their voice is not heard.

4 Their line is gone out through all the earth, and their words to the end of the world. In them hath He set a tabernacle for the sun,

5 Which is as a bridegroom coming out of his chamber, and rejoiceth as a strong man to run a race.

6 His going forth is from the end of the heaven, and his circuit unto the ends of it: and there is nothing hid from the heat thereof.

7 The law of the Lord is perfect, converting the soul: the testimony of the Lord is sure, making wise the simple.

8 The statutes of the Lord are right, rejoicing the heart: the commandment of the Lord is pure, enlightening the eyes.

9 The fear of the Lord is clean, enduring for ever: the judgments of the Lord are true and righteous altogether.

10 More to be desired are they than gold, yea, than much fine gold: sweeter also than honey and the honeycomb.

11 Moreover by them is thy servant warned: and in keeping of them there is great reward.

12 Who can understand his errors? cleanse Thou me from secret faults.

13 Keep back thy servant also from presumptuous sins; let them not have dominion over me: then shall I be upright, and I shall be innocent from the great transgression.

14 Let the words of my mouth, and the meditation of my heart, be acceptable in Thy sight, O Lord, my strength, and my Redeemer.

No. 7.   Psalm 23.

1 The Lord is my Shepherd; I shall not want.

2 He maketh me to lie down in green pastures: He leadeth me beside the still waters.

3 He restoreth my soul: He leadeth me in the paths of righteousness for His name's sake.

4 Yea, though I walk through the valley of the shadow of death, I will fear no evil: for Thou art with me; Thy rod and Thy staff they comfort me.

5 Thou preparest a table before me in the presence of mine enemies: Thou anointest my head with oil; my cup runneth over.

6 Surely goodness and mercy shall follow me all the days of my life: and I will dwell in the house of the Lord for ever.

No. 8.   Psalm 24.

1 The earth is the Lord's, and the fullness thereof; the world, and they that dwell therein.

2 For He hath founded it upon the seas, and established it upon the floods.

3 Who shall ascend into the hill of the Lord? or who shall stand in His holy place?

4 He that hath clean hands, and a pure heart; who hath not lifted up his soul unto vanity, nor sworn deceitfully.

5 He shall receive the blessing from the Lord, and righteousness from the God of his salvation.

6 This is the generation of them that seek Him, that seek Thy face, O Jacob.

7 Lift up your heads, O ye gates; and be ye lifted up, ye everlasting doors; and the King of glory shall come in.

8 Who is this King of glory? The Lord strong and mighty, the Lord mighty in battle.

9 Lift up your heads, O ye gates; even lift them up, ye everlasting doors; and the King of glory shall come in.
10 Who is this King of glory? The Lord of hosts, He is the King of glory. ·

No. 9. Psalm 46.

1 God is our refuge and strength, a very present help in trouble.
2 Therefore will not we fear, though the earth be removed, and though the mountains be carried into the midst of the sea;
3 Though the waters thereof roar and be troubled, though the mountains shake with the swelling thereof.
4 There is a river, the streams whereof shall make glad the city of God, the holy place of the tabernacles of the Most High.
5 God is in the midst of her; she shall not be moved: God shall help her, and that right early.
6 The heathen raged, the kingdoms were moved: He uttered His voice, the earth melted.
7 The Lord of hosts is with us; the God of Jacob is our refuge.
8 Come, behold the works of the Lord, what desolations He hath made in the earth.
9 He maketh wars to cease unto the end of the earth; He breaketh the bow, and cutteth the spear in sunder; He burneth the chariot in the fire.
10 Be still, and know that I am God: I will be exalted among the heathen, I will be exalted in the earth.
11 The Lord of hosts is with us; the God of Jacob is our refuge.

No. 10. Psalm 84.

1 How amiable are Thy tabernacles, O Lord of hosts!
2 My soul longeth, yea, even fainteth for the courts of the Lord: my heart and my flesh crieth out for the living God.
3 Yea, the sparrow hath found a house, and the swallow a nest for herself, where she may lay her young, even Thine altars, O Lord of hosts, my King, and my God.
4 Blessed are they that dwell in Thy house: they will be still praising Thee.
5 Blessed is the man whose strength is in Thee; in whose heart are the ways of them.
6 Who passing through the valley of Baca make it a well; the rain also filleth the pools.
7 They go from strength to strength, every one of them in Zion appeareth before God.
8 O Lord God of hosts, hear my prayer: give ear, O God of Jacob.
9 Behold, O God our shield, and look upon the face of Thine anointed.

10 For a day in Thy courts is better than a thousand. I had rather be a doorkeeper in the house of my God, than to dwell in the tents of wickedness.
11 For the Lord God is a sun and shield: the Lord will give grace and glory: no good thing will He withhold from them that walk uprightly.
12 O Lord of hosts, blessed is the man that trusteth in Thee.

No. 11. Psalm 91.

1 He that dwelleth in the secret place of the Most High shall abide under the shadow of the Almighty.
2 I will say of the Lord, He is my refuge and my fortress: my God; in Him will I trust.
3 Surely He shall deliver thee from the snare of the fowler, and from the noisome pestilence.
4 He shall cover thee with His feathers, and under His wings shalt thou trust: His truth shall be thy shield and buckler.
5 Thou shalt not be afraid for the terror by night; nor for the arrow that flieth by day;
6 Nor for the pestilence that walketh in darkness; nor for the destruction that wasteth at noonday.
7 A thousand shall fall at thy side, and ten thousand at thy right hand; but it shall not come nigh thee.
8 Only with thine eyes shalt thou behold and see the reward of the wicked.
9 Because thou hast made the Lord, which is my refuge, even the Most High, thy habitation.
10 There shall no evil befall thee, neither shall any plague come nigh thy dwelling.
11 For He shall give His angels charge over thee, to keep thee in all thy ways.
12 They shall bear thee up in their hands, lest thou dash thy foot against a stone.
13 Thou shalt tread upon the lion and adder: the young lion and the dragon shalt thou trample under feet.
14 Because he hath set his love upon me, therefore will I deliver him: I will set him on high, because he hath known my name.
15 He shall call upon me, and I will answer him: I will be with him in trouble; I will deliver him, and honor him.
16 With long life will I satisfy him, and show him my salvation.

No. 12. Psalm 103.

1 Bless the Lord, O my soul: and all that is within me, bless His holy name.
2 Bless the Lord, O my soul, and forget not all His benefits:
3 Who forgiveth all thine iniquities; who healeth all thy diseases;

4 Who redeemeth thy life from destruction; who crowneth thee with lovingkindness and tender mercies;

5 Who satisfieth thy mouth with good things; so that thy youth is renewed like the eagle's.

6 The Lord executeth righteousness and judgment for all that are oppressed.

7 He made known His ways unto Moses, His acts unto the children of Israel.

8 The Lord is merciful and gracious, slow to anger, and plenteous in mercy.

9 He will not always chide: neither will He keep His anger for ever.

10 He hath not dealt with us after our sins; nor rewarded us according to our iniquities.

11 For as the heaven is high above the earth, so great is His mercy toward them that fear Him.

12 As far as the east is from the west, so far hath He removed our transgressions from us.

No. 13.   Part 2.

13 Like as a father pitieth his children, so the Lord pitieth them that fear Him.

14 For He knoweth our frame; He remembereth that we are dust.

15 As for man, his days are as grass: as a flower of the field, so he flourisheth.

16 For the wind passeth over it, and it is gone; and the place thereof shall know it no more.

17 But the mercy of the Lord is from everlasting to everlasting upon them that fear Him, and His righteousness unto children's children;

18 To such as keep His covenant, and to those that remember His commandments to do them.

19 The Lord hath prepared His throne in the heavens; and His kingdom ruleth over all.

20 Bless the Lord, ye His angels, that excel in strength, that do His commandments, hearkening unto the voice of His word.

21 Bless ye the Lord, all ye His hosts; ye ministers of His, that do His pleasure.

22 Bless the Lord, all His works in all places of His dominion: bless the Lord, O my soul.

No. 14.   Psalm 121.

1 I will lift up mine eyes unto the hills, from whence cometh my help.

2 My help cometh from the Lord, which made heaven and earth.

3 He will not suffer thy foot to be moved: He that keepeth thee will not slumber.

4 Behold, He that keepeth Israel shall neither slumber nor sleep.

5 The Lord is thy keeper: the Lord is thy shade upon thy right hand.

6 The sun shall not smite thee by day, nor the moon by night.

7 The Lord shall preserve thee from all evil: He shall preserve thy soul.

8 The Lord shall preserve thy going out and thy coming in from this time forth, and even for evermore.

No. 15.   Psalm 122.

1 I was glad when they said unto me, Let us go into the house of the Lord.

2 Our feet shall stand within thy gates, O Jerusalem.

3 Jerusalem is builded as a city that is compact together:

4 Whither the tribes go up, the tribes of the Lord, unto the testimony of Israel, to give thanks unto the name of the Lord.

5 For there are set thrones of judgment, the thrones of the house of David.

6 Pray for the peace of Jerusalem: they shall prosper that love thee.

7 Peace be within thy walls, and prosperity within thy palaces.

8 For my brethren and companions' sakes, I will now say, Peace be within thee.

9 Because of the house of the Lord our God I will seek thy good.

No. 16.   Prov. 3.

1 to 17.

1 My son, forget not my law; but let thine heart keep my commandments:

2 For length of days, and long life, and peace, shall they add to thee.

3 Let not mercy and truth forsake thee: bind them about thy neck; write them upon the table of thine heart:

4 So shalt thou find favor and good understanding in the sight of God and man.

5 Trust in the Lord with all thine heart; and lean not unto thine own understanding.

6 In all thy ways acknowledge Him, and He shall direct thy paths.

7 Be not wise in thine own eyes: fear the Lord, and depart from evil.

8 It shall be health to thy navel, and marrow to thy bones.

9 Honor the Lord with thy substance, and with the first fruits of all thine increase:

10 So shall thy barns be filled with plenty, and thy presses shall burst out with new wine.

11 My son, despise not the chastening of the Lord; neither be weary of His correction;

12 For whom the Lord loveth He correcteth; even as a father the son in whom he delighteth.

13 Happy is the man that findeth wisdom, and the man that getteth understanding.

14 For the merchandise of it is better than the merchandise of silver, and the gain thereof than fine gold.

15 She is more precious than rubies: and all the things thou canst desire are not to be compared unto her.

16 Length of days is in her right hand; and in her left hand riches and honor.

17 Her ways are ways of pleasantness, and all her paths are peace.

No. 17. Remember Thy Creator.
Eccle. 12, 1-14.

1 Remember now thy Creator in the days of thy youth, while the evil days come not, nor the years draw nigh, when thou shalt say, I have no pleasure in them;

2 While the sun, or the light, or the moon, or the stars, be not darkened, nor the clouds return after the rain:

3 In the day when the keepers of the house shall tremble, and the strong men shall bow themselves, and the grinders cease because they are few, and those that look out of the windows be darkened,

4 And the doors shall be shut in the streets, when the sound of grinding is low, and He shall rise up at the voice of the bird, and all the daughters of music shall be brought low;

5 Also when they shall be afraid of that which is high, and fears shall be in the way, and the almond tree shall flourish, and the grasshopper shall be a burden, and desire shall fail: because man goeth to his long home, and the mourners go about the streets:

6 Or ever the silver cord be loosed, or the golden bowl be broken, or the pitcher be broken at the fountain, or the wheel broken at the cistern.

7 Then shall the dust return to the earth as it was: and the spirit shall return unto God who gave it.

8 Vanity of vanities, saith the preacher; all is vanity.

9 And moreover, because the preacher was wise, he still taught the people knowledge; yea, he gave good heed, and sought out, and set in order many proverbs.

10 The preacher sought to find out acceptable words: and that which was written was upright, even words of truth.

11 The words of the wise are as goads, and as nails fastened by the masters of assemblies, which are given from one shepherd.

12 And further, by these, my son, be admonished: of making many books there is no end; and much study is a weariness of the flesh.

13 Let us hear the conclusion of the whole matter: Fear God, and keep His commandments: for this is the whole duty of man.

14 For God shall bring every work into judgment, with every secret thing, whether it be good, or whether it be evil.

No. 18. The Beatitudes.

Blessed are the poor in spirit: for theirs is the kingdom of heaven.

Blessed are they that mourn: for they shall be comforted.

Blessed are the meek: for they shall inherit the earth.

Blessed are they which do hunger and thirst after righteousness: for they shall be filled.

Blessed are the merciful: for they shall obtain mercy.

Blessed are the pure in heart: for they shall see God.

Blessed are the peacemakers: for they shall be called the children of God.

Blessed are they which are persecuted for righteousness' sake: for theirs is the kingdom of heaven.

Blessed are ye, when men shall revile you, and persecute you, and shall say all manner of evil against you falsely, for my sake.

Rejoice, and be exceeding glad: for great is your reward in heaven: for so persecuted they the prophets which were before you.

No. 19. The Word.
St. John 1, 1-18.

1 In the beginning was the Word, and the Word was with God, and the Word was God.

2 The same was in the beginning with God.

3 All things were made by Him; and without Him was not anything made that was made.

4 In Him was life; and the life was the light of men.

5 And the light shineth in darkness; and the darkness comprehended it not.

6 There was a man sent from God, whose name was John.

7 The same came for a witness, to bear witness of the Light, that all men through him might believe.

8 He was not that Light, but was sent to bear witness of that Light.

9 That was the true Light, which lighteth every man that cometh into the world.

10 He was in the world, and the world was made by Him, and the world knew Him not.

11 He came unto His own, and His own received Him not.

12 But as many as received Him, to them gave He power to become the sons of God, even to them that believe on His name:

13 Which were born, not of blood, nor of the will of the flesh, nor of the will of man, but of God.

14 And the Word was made flesh, and dwelt among us, (and we beheld His glory, the glory as of the only begotten of the Father,) full of grace and truth.

15 John bare witness of Him, and cried, saying, This was He of whom I spake, He that cometh after me is preferred before me: for He was before me.

16 And of His fullness have all we received, and grace for grace.

17 For the law was given by Moses, but grace and truth came by Jesus Christ.

18 No man hath seen God at any time; the only begotten Son, which is in the bosom of the Father, He hath declared Him.

No. 20.   Charity.

1st. Cor. 13.

1 Though I speak with the tongues of men and of angels, and have not charity, I am become as sounding brass, or a tinkling cymbal.

2 And though I have the gift of prophecy, and understand all mysteries, and all knowledge; and though I have all faith, so that I could remove mountains, and have not charity, I am nothing.

3 And though I bestow all my goods to feed the poor, and though I give my body to be burned, and have not charity, it profiteth me nothing.

4 Charity suffereth long, and is kind; charity envieth not; charity vaunteth not itself, is not puffed up.

5 Doth not behave itself unseemly, seeketh not her own, is not easily provoked, thinketh no evil;

6 Rejoiceth not in iniquity, but rejoiceth in the truth;

7 Beareth all things, believeth all things, hopeth all things, endureth all things.

8 Charity never faileth: but whether there be prophecies, they shall fail; whether there be tongues, they shall cease; whether there be knowledge, it shall vanish away.

9 For we know in part, and we prophesy in part.

10 But when that which is perfect is come, then that which is in part shall be done away.

11 When I was a child, I spake as a child, I understood as a child, I thought as a child: but when I became a man, I put away childish things.

12 For now we see through a glass, darkly; but then face to face: now I know in part; but then shall I know even as also I am known.

13 And now abideth faith, hope, charity, these three; but the greatest of these is charity.

No. 21.   The Christian Soldier.

Eph. 6, 10-17.

10 Finally, my brethren, be strong in the Lord, and in the power of His might.

11 Put on the whole armor of God, that ye may be able to stand against the wiles of the devil.

12 For we wrestle not against flesh and blood, but against principalities, against powers, against the rulers of the darkness of this world, against spiritual wickedness in high places.

13 Wherefore take unto you the whole armor of God, that ye may be able to withstand in the evil day, and having done all, to stand.

14 Stand therefore, having your loins girt about with truth, and having on the breastplate of righteousness;

15 And your feet shod with the preparation of the gospel of peace;

16 Above all, taking the shield of faith, wherewith ye shall be able to quench all the fiery darts of the wicked.

17 And take the helmet of salvation, and the sword of the Spirit, which is the word of God:

No. 22.   Pure Religion.

James 1, 22-27.

22 But be ye doers of the word, and not hearers only, deceiving your own selves.

23 For if any be a hearer of the word, and not a doer, he is like unto a man beholding his natural face in a glass:

24 For he beholdeth himself, and goeth his way, and straightway forgetteth what manner of man he was.

25 But whoso looketh into the perfect law of liberty, and continueth therein, he being not a forgetful hearer, but a doer of the work, this man shall be blessed in his deed.

26 If any man among you seem to be religious, and bridleth not his tongue, but deceiveth his own heart, this man's religion is vain.

27 Pure religion and undefiled before God and the Father is this, To visit the fatherless and widows in their affliction, and to keep himself unspotted from the world.

No. 23.   Confidence in God.   *Psalm 42.*

1 As the hart panteth after the water brooks, so panteth my soul after thee, O God.

2 My soul thirsteth for God, for the living God: when shall I come and appear before God?

3 My tears have been my meat day and night, while they continually say unto me, Where is thy God?

4 When I remember these things, I pour out my soul in me: for I had gone with the multitude, I went with them to the house of God, with the voice of joy and praise, with a multitude that kept holyday.

5 Why art thou cast down, O my soul? and why art thou disquieted in me? hope thou in God: for I shall yet praise him for the help of his countenance.

6 O my God, my soul is cast down within me: therefore will I remember thee from the land of Jordan, and of the Hermonites, from the hill Mizar.

7 Deep calleth unto deep at the noise of thy waterspouts: all thy waves and thy billows are gone over me.

8 Yet the Lord will command his lovingkindness in the daytime, and in the night his song shall be with me, and my prayer unto the God of my life.

9 I will say unto God my rock, Why hast thou forgotten me? why go I mourning because of the oppression of the enemy?

10 As with a sword in my bones, mine enemies reproach me; while they say daily unto me, Where is thy God?

11 Why art thou cast down, O my soul? and why art thou disquieted within me? hope thou in God; for I shall yet praise him, who is the health of my countenance, and my God.

No. 24.   Trust in the Lord.   *Psalm 115.*

1 Not unto us, O Lord, not unto us, but unto thy name give glory, for thy mercy, and for thy truth's sake.

2 Wherefore should the heathen say, Where is now their God?

3 But our God is in the heavens: he hath done whatsoever he hath pleased. ·

4 Their idols are silver and gold, the work of men's hands.

5 They have mouths, but they speak not: eyes have they, but they see not:

6 They have ears, but they hear not: noses have they, but they smell not:

7 They have hands, but they handle not: feet have they, but they walk not: neither speak they through their throat.

8 They that make them are like unto them; so is every one that trusteth in them.

9 O Israel, trust thou in the Lord: he is their help and their shield.

10 O house of Aaron, trust in the Lord: he is their help and their shield.

11 Ye that fear the Lord, trust in the Lord: he is their help and their shield.

12 The Lord hath been mindful of us: he will bless us; he will bless the house of Israel; he will bless the house of Aaron.

13 He will bless them that fear the Lord, both small and great.

14 The Lord shall increase you more and more, you and your children.

15 Ye are blessed of the Lord which made heaven and earth.

16 The heaven, even the heavens, are the Lord's: but the earth hath he given to the children of men.

17 The dead praise not the Lord, neither any that go down into silence.

18 But we will bless the Lord from this time forth and for evermore. Praise the Lord.

No. 25.   Wisdom.   *Prov. 4, 1–13.*

1 Hear, ye children, the instruction of a father, and attend to know understanding.

2 For I give you good doctrine, forsake ye not my law.

3 For I was my father's son, tender and only beloved in the sight of my mother.

4 He taught me also, and said unto me, Let thine heart retain my words: keep my commandments, and live.

5 Get wisdom, get understanding: forget it not; neither decline from the words of my mouth.

6 Forsake her not, and she shall preserve thee: love her, and she shall keep thee.

7 Wisdom is the principal thing; therefore get wisdom: and with all thy getting get understanding.

8 Exalt her, and she shall promote thee: she shall bring thee to honour, when thou dost embrace her.

9 She shall give to thine head an ornament of grace: a crown of glory shall she deliver to thee.

10 Hear, O my son, and receive my sayings; and the years of thy life shall be many.

11 I have taught thee in the way of wisdom; I have led thee in right paths.

12 When thou goest, thy steps shall not be straitened; and when thou runnest, thou shalt not stumble.

13 Take fast hold of instruction; let her not go: keep her; for she is thy life.

No. 26.   ·   Temperance.

Proverbs XX.

1 Wine is a mocker, strong drink is raging: and whosoever is deceived thereby is not wise.

Proverbs XXI.

17 He that loveth pleasure shall be a poor man: he that loveth wine and oil shall not be rich.

Proverbs XXIII.

19 Hear thou, my son, and be wise, and guide thine heart in the way.

20 Be not among winebibbers; among riotous eaters of flesh:

21 For the drunkard and the glutton shall come to poverty: and drowsiness shall clothe a man with rags.

29 Who hath woe? who hath sorrow? who hath contentions? who hath babblings? who hath wounds without cause? who hath redness of eyes?

30 They that tarry long at the wine: they that go to seek mixed wine.

31 Look not thou upon the wine when it is red, when it giveth his colour in the cup, when it moveth itself aright.

32 At the last it biteth like a serpent, and stingeth like an adder.

Galatians V.

19 Now the works of the flesh are manifest, which are these; * * *

21 Envyings, murders, drunkenness, revellings, and such like: of the which I tell you before, as I have also told you in time past, that they which do such things shall not inherit the kingdom of God.

22 But the fruit of the Spirit is love, joy, peace, long suffering, gentleness, goodness, faith.

23 Meekness, temperance: against such there is no law.

II Peter I.

5 And besides this, giving all diligence, add to your faith virtue; and to virtue knowledge;

6 And to knowledge temperance; and to temperance patience; and to patience godliness;

7 And to godliness brotherly kindness; and to brotherly kindness charity.

No. 27.   Temperance.   *Isaiah 5, 11-23.*

11 Woe unto them that rise up early in the morning, that they may follow strong drink; that continue until night, till wine inflame them!

12 And the harp and the viol, the tabret and pipe, and wine, are in their feasts: but they regard not the work of the Lord, neither consider the operation of his hands.

13 Therefore my people are gone into captivity, because they have no knowledge: and their honourable men are famished, and their multitude dried up with thirst.

14 Therefore hell hath enlarged herself, and opened her mouth without measure: and their glory, and their multitude, and their pomp, and he that rejoiceth, shall descend into it.

15 And the mean man shall be brought down, and the mighty man shall be humbled, and the eyes of the lofty shall be humbled:

16 But the Lord of hosts shall be exalted in judgment, and God that is holy shall be sanctified in righteousness.

17 Then shall the lambs feed after their manner, and the waste places of the fat ones shall strangers eat.

18 Woe unto them that draw iniquity with cords of vanity, and sin as it were with a cart rope:

19 That say, Let him make speed, and hasten his work, that we may see it: and let the counsel of the Holy One of Israel draw nigh and come, that we may know it.

20 Woe unto them that call evil good, and good evil; that put darkness for light, and light for darkness; that put bitter for sweet, and sweet for bitter!

21 Woe unto them that are wise in their own eyes, and prudent in their own sight!

22 Woe unto them that are mighty to drink wine, and men of strength to mingle strong drink:

23 Which justify the wicked for reward, and take away the righteousness of the righteous from him!

No. 28.   Invitation.   *Isaiah 55. 1-13.*

1 Ho, every one that thirsteth, come ye to the waters, and he that hath no money; come ye, buy and eat; yea, come, buy wine and milk without money and without price.

2 Wherefore do ye spend money for that which is not bread? and your labor for that which satisfieth not? hearken diligently unto me, and eat ye that which is good, and let your soul delight itself in fatness.

3 Incline your ear, and come unto me; hear, and your soul shall live; and I will make an everlasting covenant with you, even the sure mercies of David.

4 Behold, I have given him for a witness to the people, a leader and commander to the people.

5 Behold, thou shalt call a nation that thou knowest not, and nations that knew not

thee shall run unto thee because of the Lord thy God, and for the Holy One of Israel; for he hath glorified thee.

6 Seek ye the Lord while he may be found, call ye upon him while he is near:

7 Let the wicked forsake his way, and the unrighteousness man his thoughts: and let him return unto the Lord, and he will have mercy upon him; and to our God, for he will abundantly pardon.

8 For my thoughts are not your thoughts, neither are your ways my ways, saith the Lord.

9 For as the heavens are higher than the earth, so are my ways higher than your ways, and my thoughts than your thoughts.

10 For as the rain cometh down, and the snow from heaven, and returneth not thither, but watereth the earth, and maketh it bring forth and bud, that it may give seed to the sower, and bread to the eater:

11 So shall my word be that goeth forth out of my mouth: it shall not return unto me void, but it shall accomplish that which I please, and it shall prosper in the thing whereto I sent it.

12 For ye shall go out with joy, and be led forth with peace: the mountains and the hills shall break forth before you into singing, and all the trees of the field shall clap their hands.

13 Instead of the thorn shall come up the fir tree, and instead of the brier shall come up the myrtle tree: and it shall be to the Lord for a name, for an everlasting sign that shall not be cut off.

No. 29.   Resist Not Evil.   *Matt. 5, 38-48.*

38 Ye have heard that it hath been said, An eye for an eye, and a tooth for a tooth:

39 But I say unto you, That ye resist not evil: but whosoever shall smite thee on thy right cheek, turn to him the other also.

40 And if any man will sue thee at the law, and take away thy coat, let him have thy cloak also.

41 And whosoever shall compel thee to go a mile, go with him twain.

42 Give to him that asketh thee, and from him that would borrow of thee turn not thou away.

43 Ye have heard that it hath been said, Thou shalt love thy neighbour, and hate thine enemy.

44 But I say unto you, Love your enemies, bless them that curse you, do good to them that hate you, and pray for them which despitefully use you, and persecute you;

45 That ye may be the children of your Father which is in heaven: for he maketh his sun to rise on the evil and on the good, and sendeth rain on the just and on the unjust.

46 For if ye love them which love you, what reward have ye? do not even the publicans the same?

47 And if ye salute your brethren only, what do ye more than others? do not even the publicans so?

48 Be ye therefore perfect, even as your Father which is in heaven is perfect.

No. 30.   Heavenly Treasures.   *Matt. 6. 19-34.*

19 Lay not up for yourselves treasures upon earth, where moth and rust doth corrupt, and where thieves break through and steal:

20 But lay up for yourselves treasures in heaven, where neither moth nor rust doth corrupt, and where thieves do not break through nor steal.

21 For where your treasure is, there will your heart be also.

22 The light of the body is the eye: if therefore thine eye be single, thy whole body shall be full of light.

23 But if thine eye be evil, thy whole body shall be full of darkness. If therefore the light that is in thee be darkness, how great is that darkness?

24 No man can serve two masters: for either he will hate the one, and love the other; or else he will hold to the one, and despise the other. Ye cannot serve God and mammon.

25 Therefore I say unto you, Take no thought for your life, what ye shall eat, or what ye shall drink: nor yet for your body, what ye shall put on. Is not the life more than meat, and and the body than raiment?

26 Behold the fowls of the air: for they sow not, neither do they reap, nor gather into barns: yet your heavenly Father feedeth them. Are ye not much better than they?

27 Which of you by taking thought can add one cubit unto his stature?

28 And why take ye thought for raiment? Consider the lilies of the field, how they grow: they toil not, neither do they spin:

29 And yet I say unto you, That even Solomon in all his glory was not arrayed like one of these.

30 Wherefore, if God so clothe the grass of the field, which to-day is and to-morrow is cast into the oven, shall he not much more clothe you, O ye of little faith?

31 Therefore take no thought, saying, What shall we eat? or, What shall we drink? or, Wherewithal shall we be clothed?

32 (For after all these things do the Gentiles seek:) for your heavenly Father knoweth that ye have need of all these things.

33 But seek ye first the kingdom of God, and his righteousness; and all these things shall be added unto you.

34 Take therefore no thought for the morrow: for the morrow shall take thought for the things of itself. Sufficient unto the day is the evil thereof.

No. 31. Golden Rule. *Matt. 7, 1-12.*

1 Judge not, that ye be not judged.

2 For with what judgment ye judge ye shall be judged: and with what measure ye mete, it shall be measured to you again.

3 And why beholdest thou the mote that is in thy brother's eye, but considerest not the beam that is in thine own eye?

4 Or how wilt thou say to thy brother, Let me pull out the mote out of thine eye; and, behold, a beam is in thine own eye?

5 Thou hypocrite, first cast out the beam out of thine own eye: and then shalt thou see clearly to cast out the mote out of thy brother's eye.

6 Give not that which is holy unto the dogs, neither cast ye your pearls before swine, lest they trample them under their feet: and turn again and rend you.

7 Ask, and it shall be given you; seek, and ye shall find; knock, and it shall be opened unto you.

8 For every one that asketh receiveth; and he that seeketh findeth; and to him that knocketh it shall be opened.

9 Or what man is there of you, whom if his son ask bread, will he give him a stone?

10 Or if he ask a fish, will he give him a serpent?

11 If ye then, being evil, know how to give good gifts unto your children, how much more shall your Father, which is in heaven, give good things to them that ask him?

12 Therefore all things whatsoever ye would that men should do to you, do ye even so to them: for this is the law and the prophets.

No. 32. Parable of the Sower. *Matt. 13. 1-9; 18-23.*

1 The same day went Jesus out of the house, and sat by the sea side.

2 And great multitudes were gathered together unto him, so that he went into a ship, and sat; and the whole multitude stood on the shore.

3 And he spake many things unto them in parables, saying, Behold, a sower went forth to sow;

4 And when he sowed, some seeds fell by the way side, and the fowls came and devoured them up:

5 Some fell upon stony places, where they had not much earth: and forthwith they sprung up, because they had no deepness of earth:

6 And when the sun was up, they were scorched; and because they had no root, they withered away.

7 And some fell among thorns; and the thorns sprung up, and choked them:

8 But others fell into good ground, and brought forth fruit, some an hundredfold, some sixtyfold, some thirtyfold.

9 Who hath ears to hear, let him hear.

18 Hear ye therefore the parable of the sower.

19 When any one heareth the word of the kingdom, and understandeth it not, then cometh the wicked one, and catcheth away that which was sown in his heart. This is he which received seed by the way side.

20 But he that received the seed into stony places, the same is he that heareth the word, and anon with joy receiveth it;

21 Yet hath he not root in himself, but dureth for a while: for when tribulation or persecution ariseth because of the word, by and by he is offended.

22 He also that received seed among the thorns is he that heareth the word; and the care of this world, and the deceitfulness of richness, choke the word, and he becometh unfruitful.

23 But he that received seed into the good ground is he that heareth the word, and understandeth it; which also beareth fruit, and bringeth forth, some an hundredfold, some sixty, some thirty.

No. 33. Parable of the Ten Virgins. *Matt. 25. 1-13.*

1 Then shall the kingdom of heaven be likened unto ten virgins, which took their lamps, and went forth to meet the bridegroom.

2 And five of them were wise, and five were foolish.

3 They that were foolish took their lamps, and took no oil with them:

4 But the wise took oil in their vessels with their lamps.

5 While the bridegroom tarried, they all slumbered and slept.

6 And at midnight there was a cry made, Behold, the bridegroom cometh; go ye out to meet him.

7 Then all those virgins arose, and trimmed their lamps.

8 And the foolish said unto the wise, Give

us of your oil; for our lamps are gone out. was shut.

9 But the wise answered, saying, Not so; lest there be not enough for us and you: but go ye rather to them that sell, and buy for yourselves.

10 And while they went to buy, the bridegroom came: and they that were ready went in with him to the marriage: and the door was shut.

11 Afterward came also the other virgins, saying, Lord, Lord, open to us.

12 But he answered and said, Verily I say unto you, I know you not.

13 Watch, therefore, for ye know neither the day nor the hour wherein the Son of man cometh.

No. 34.   Parable of the Ten Talents. *Matt. 25. 14-29.*

14 For the kingdom of heaven is as a man travelling into a far country, who called his own servants, and delivered unto them his goods.

15 And unto one he gave five talents, to another two, and to another one; to every man according to his several ability; and straightway took his journey.

16 Then he that had received the five talents went and traded with the same, and made them other five talents.

17 And likewise he that had received two, he also gained other two.

18 But he that had received one went and digged in the earth, and hid his lord's money.

19 After a long time the lord of those servants cometh, and reckoneth with them.

20 And so he that had received five talents came and brought other five talents, saying, Lord, thou deliveredst unto me five talents: behold, I have gained besides them five talents more.

21 His lord said unto him, Well done, thou good and faithful servant: thou hast been faithful over a few things, I will make thee ruler over many things: enter thou into the joy of thy lord.

22 He also that had received two talents came and said, Lord, thou deliveredst unto me two talents: behold, I have gained two other talents besides them.

23 His lord said unto him, Well done, good and faithful servant: thou hast been faithful over a few things, I will make thee ruler over many things; enter thou into the joy of thy lord.

24 Then he which had received the one talent came and said, Lord, I knew thee that thou art an hard man, reaping where thou hast not sown, and gathering where thou hast not strawed:

25 And I was afraid, and went and hid thy talent in the earth: lo, there thou hast that is thine.

26 His lord answered and said unto him, Thou wicked and slothful servant, thou knewest that I reap where I sowed not, and gather where I have not strawed:

27 Thou oughtest therefore to have put my money to the exchangers, and then at my coming I should have received mine own with usury.

28 Take therefore the talent from him, and give it unto him which hath ten talents.

29 For unto every one that hath shall be given, and he shall have abundance: but from him that hath not shall be taken away even that which he hath.

No. 35.   John the Baptist's Witness to Jesus. *John 1. 19-34.*

19 And this is the record of John, when the Jews sent priests and Levites from Jerusalem to ask him, Who art thou?

20 And he confessed, and denied not; but confessed, I am not the Christ.

21 And they asked him, What then? Art thou Elias? And he saith, I am not. Art thou that Prophet? And he answered, No.

22 Then said they unto him, Who art thou? that we may give an answer to them that sent us. What sayest thou of thyself?

23 He said, I am the voice of one crying in the wilderness, Make straight the way of the Lord, as said the prophet Esaias.

24 And they which were sent were of the Pharisees.

25 And they asked him, and said unto him, Why baptizest thou then, if thou be not that Christ, nor Elias, neither that Prophet?

26 John answered them, saying, I baptize with water: but there standeth one among you, whom ye know not;

27 He it is, who coming after me is preferred before me, whose shoe's latchet I am not worthy to unloose.

28 These things were done in Bethabara beyond Jordan, where John was baptizing.

29 The next day John seeth Jesus coming unto him, and saith, Behold the Lamb of God, which taketh away the sin of the world!

30 This is he of whom I said, After me cometh a man which is preferred before me; for he was before me.

31 And I knew him not: but that he should be made manifest to Israel, therefore am I come baptizing with water.

32 And John bare record, saying, I saw the Spirit descending from heaven like a dove, and it abode upon him.

33 And I knew him not: but he that sent me to baptize with water, the same said unto me, Upon whom thou shalt see the Spirit descending, and remaining on him, the same is he which baptizeth with the Holy Ghost.

34 And I saw, and bare record that this is the Son of God.

No. 36. The Twelve Apostles Chosen. *Luke 6. 12-23.*

12 And it came to pass in those days, that he went out into a mountain to pray, and continued all night in prayer to God.

13 And when it was day, he called unto him his disciples; and of them he chose twelve, whom also he named apostles;

14 Simon, (whom he also named Peter,) and Andrew his brother, James and John, Philip and Bartholomew,

15 Matthew and Thomas, James the son of Alpheus, and Simon called Zelotes,

16 And Judas the brother of James, and Judas Iscariot, which also was the traitor.

17 And he came down with them, and stood in the plain, and the company of his disciples, and a great multitude of people out of all Judea and Jerusalem, and from the sea coast of Tyre and Sidon, which came to hear him, and to be healed of their diseases;

18 And they that were vexed with unclean spirits: and they were healed.

19 And the whole multitude sought to touch him: for there went virtue out of him, and he healed them all.

20 And he lifted up his eyes on his disciples, and said, Blessed be ye poor: for yours is the kingdom of God.

21 Blessed are ye that hunger now: for ye shall be filled. Blessed are ye that weep now: for ye shall laugh.

22 Blessed are ye, when men shall hate you, and when they shall separate you from their company, and shall reproach you, and cast out your name as evil, for the Son of man's sake.

23 Rejoice ye in that day, and leap for joy: for, behold, your reward is great in heaven: for in the like manner did their fathers unto the prophets.

No. 37. Parable of the Good Samaritan. *Luke 10. 25-37.*

25 And, behold, a certain lawyer stood up, and tempted him, saying, Master, what shall I do to inherit eternal life?

26 He said unto him, What is written in the law? how readest thou?

27 And he answering said, Thou shalt love the Lord thy God with all thy heart, and with all thy soul, and with all thy strength, and with all thy mind; and thy neighbour as thyself.

28 And he said unto him, Thou hast answered right: this do, and thou shalt live.

29 But he, willing to justify himself, said unto Jesus, And who is my neighbour?

30 And Jesus answering said, a certain man went down from Jerusalem to Jericho, and fell among thieves, which stripped him of his raiment, and wounded him, and departed, leaving him half dead.

31 And by chance there came down a certain priest that way; and when he saw him, he passed by on the other side.

32 And likewise a Levite, when he was at the place, came and looked on him, and passed by on the other side.

33 But a certain Samaritan, as he journeyed, came where he was; and when he saw him, he had compassion on him,

34 And went to him, and bound up his wounds, pouring in oil and wine, and set him on his own beast, and brought him to an inn, and took care of him.

35 And on the morrow when he departed, he took out two pence, and gave them to the host, and said unto him, Take care of him: and whatsoever thou spendest more, when I come again, I will repay thee.

36 Which now of these three, thinkest thou, was neighbour unto him that fell among the thieves?

37 And he said, He that shewed mercy on him. Then said Jesus unto him, Go, and do thou likewise.

No. 38. The Great Refusal. *Luke 18. 18-30.*

18 And a certain ruler asked him, saying, Good Master, what shall I do to inherit eternal life?

19 And Jesus said unto him, Why callest thou me good? none is good, save one, that is, God.

20 Thou knowest the commandments, Do not commit adultery, Do not kill, Do not steal, Do not bear false witness, Honour thy father and thy mother.

21 And he said, All these have I kept from my youth up.

22 Now when Jesus heard these things, he said unto him, Yet lackest thou one thing: sell all that thou hast, and distribute unto the poor, and thou shalt have treasure in heaven: and come, follow me.

23 And when he heard this, he was very sorrowful: for he was very rich.

24 And when Jesus saw that he was very

sorrowful, he said, How hardly shall they that have riches enter into the kingdom of God!

25 For it is easier for a camel to go through a needle's eye, than for a rich man to enter into the kingdom of God.

26 And they that heard it said, Who then can be saved?

27 And he said, The things which are impossible with men are possible with God.

28 Then Peter said, Lo, we have left all, and followed thee.

29 And he said unto them, Verily I say unto you, There is no man that hath left house, or parents, or brethren, or wife, or children, for the kingdom of God's sake,

30 Who shall not receive manifold more in this present time, and in the world to come life everlasting.

No. 39. The Last Judgment. *Matt. 25, 31–46.*

31 When the Son of man shall come in his glory, and all the holy angels with him, then shall he sit upon the throne of his glory:

32 And before him shall be gathered all nations: and he shall separate them one from another, as a shepherd divideth his sheep from the goats:

33 And he shall set the sheep on his right hand, but the goats on the left.

34 Then shall the King say unto them on his right hand, Come, ye blessed of my Father, inherit the kingdom prepared for you from the foundation of the world:

35 For I was a hungered, and ye gave me meat: I was thirsty, and ye gave me drink: I was a stranger, and ye took me in:

36 Naked, and ye clothed me: I was sick, and ye visited me: I was in prison, and ye came unto me.

37 Then shall the righteous answer him, saying, Lord, when saw we thee a hungered, and fed thee? or thirsty, and gave thee drink?

38 When saw we thee a stranger, and took thee in? or naked, and clothed thee?

39 Or when saw we thee sick, or in prison,

and came unto thee?

40 And the King shall answer and say unto them, Verily I say unto you, Inasmuch as ye have done it unto one of the least of these my brethren, ye have done it unto me.

41 Then shall he say also unto them on the left hand, Depart from me, ye cursed, into everlasting fire, prepared for the devil and his angels:

42 For I was a hungered, and ye gave me no meat: I was thirsty, and ye gave me no drink:

43 I was a stranger, and ye took me not in: naked, and ye clothed me not: sick, and in prison, and ye visited me not.

44 Then shall they also answer him, saying, Lord, when saw we thee a hungered, or athirst, or a stranger, or naked, or sick, or in prison, and did not minister unto thee?

45 Then shall he answer them, saying, Verily I say unto you, Inasmuch as ye did it not to one of the least of these, ye did it not to me.

46 And these shall go away into everlasting punishment: but the righteous into life eternal.

No. 40. Paul at Athens. *Acts 17, 19–31.*

19 And they took him, and brought him unto Areopagus, saying May we know what this new doctrine, whereof thou speakest, is?

20 For thou bringest certain strange things to our ears; we would know therefore what these things mean.

21 (For all the Athenians and strangers which were there spent their time in nothing else, but either to tell, or to hear some new thing.)

22 Then Paul stood in the midst of Mars' hill, and said, Ye men of Athens, I perceive that in all things ye are too superstitious.

23 For as I passed by, and beheld your devotions, I found an altar with this inscription, TO THE UNKNOWN GOD. Whom therefore ye ignorantly worship, him declare I unto you.

24 God that made the world and all things therein, seeing that he is Lord of heaven and earth, dwelleth not in temples made with hands;

25 Neither is worshiped with men's hands, as though he needed any thing, seeing he

giveth to all life, and breath, and all things;

26 And hath made of one blood all nations of men for to dwell on all ths face of the earth, and hath determined the times before appointed, and the bounds of their habitation;

27 That they should seek the Lord, if haply they might feel after him, and find him, though he be not far from every one of us:

28 For in him we live, and move, and have our being; as certain also of your own poets have said, For we are also his offspring.

29 Forasmuch then as we are the offspring of God, we ought not to think that the Godhead is like unto gold, or silver, or stone, graven by art and man's device.

30 And the times of this ignorance God winked at; but now commandeth all men every where to repent.

31 Because he hath appointed a day, in the which he will judge the world in righteousness by that man whom he hath ordained; whereof he hath given assurance unto all men, in that he hath raised him from the dead.

No. 41. The Great Doctrine. Rom. 5. 1-11.

1 Therefore being justified by faith, we have peace with God through our Lord Jesus Christ:

2 By whom also we have access by faith into this grace wherein we stand, and rejoice in hope of the glory of God.

3 And not only so, but we glory in tribulations also; knowing that tribulation worketh patience;

4 And patience, experience; and experience, hope:

5 And hope maketh not ashamed; because the love of God is shed abroad in our hearts by the Holy Ghost which is given unto us.

6 For when we were yet without strength, in due time Christ died for the ungodly.

7 For scarcely for a righteous man will one die: yet peradventure for a good man some would even dare to die.

8 But God commendeth his love toward us, in that, while we were yet sinners, Christ died for us.

9 Much more then, being now justified by his blood, we shall be saved from wrath through him.

10 For if, when we were enemies, we were reconciled to God by the death of his Son; much more, being reconciled, we shall be saved by his life.

11 And not only so, but we also joy in God through our Lord Jesus Christ, by whom we have now received the atonement.

No. 42. Sundry Exhortations. Rom. 12. 1-21.

1 I beseech you therefore, brethren, by the mercies of God, that ye present your bodies a living sacrifice, holy, acceptable unto God, which is your reasonable service.

2 And be not conformed to this world: but be ye transformed by the renewing of your mind, that ye may prove what is that good, and acceptable, and perfect will of God.

3 For I say, through the grace given unto me, to every man that is among you, not to think of himself more highly than he ought to think; but to think soberly, according as God hath dealt to every man the measure of faith.

4 For as we have many members in one body, and all members have not the same office:

5 So we, being many, are one body in Christ, and every one members one of another.

6 Having then gifts differing according to the grace that is given to us, whether prophecy, let us prophesy according to the proportion of faith;

7 Or ministry, let us wait on our ministering; or he that teacheth, on teaching;

8 Or he that exhorteth, on exhortation: he that giveth, let him do it with simplicity; he that ruleth, with diligence; he that sheweth mercy, with cheerfulness.

9 Let love be without dissimulation. Abhor that which is evil; cleave to that which is good.

10 Be kindly affectioned one to another with brotherly love; in honour preferring one another;

11 Not slothful in business; fervent in spirit; serving the Lord;

12 Rejoicing in hope; patient in tribulation; continuing instant in prayer;

13 Distributing to the necessity of saints; given to hospitality.

14 Bless them which persecute you: bless and curse not.

15 Rejoice with them that do rejoice, and weep with them that weep.

16 Be of the same mind one toward another. Mind not high things, but condescend to men of low estate. Be not wise in your own conceits.

17 Recompense to no man evil for evil. Provide things honest in the sight of all men.

18 If it be possible, as much as lieth in you, live peaceably with all men.

19 Dearly beloved, avenge not yourselves, but rather give place unto wrath: for it is written, Vengeance is mine; I will repay, saith the Lord.

20 Therefore if thine enemy hunger, feed him; if he thirst, give him drink: for in so doing thou shalt heap coals of fire on his head.

21 Be not overcome of evil, but overcome evil with good.

No. 43. Our Civil Duties. Rom. 13. 1-8.

1 Let every soul be subject unto the higher powers. For there is no power but of God: the powers that be are ordained of God.

2 Whosoever therefore resisteth the power, resisteth the ordinance of God: and they that resist shall receive to themselves damnation.

3 For rulers are not a terror to good works, but to the evil. Wilt thou then not be afraid of the power? do that which is good, and thou shalt have praise of the same:

4 For he is the minister of God to thee for good. But if thou do that which is evil, be afraid; for he beareth not the sword in vain;

for he is the minister of God, a revenger to execute wrath upon him that doeth evil.

5 Wherefore ye must needs be subject, not only for wrath, but also for conscience sake.

6 For for this cause pay ye tribute also; for they are God's ministers, attending continually upon this very thing.

7 Render therefore to all their dues; tribute to whom tribute is due; custom to whom custom; fear to whom fear: honour to whom honour.

8 Owe no man anything, but to love one another; for he that loveth another hath fulfilled the law.

No. 44. The Only Foundation. *I Cor. 3. 1-11, 21-23.*

1 And I, brethren, could not speak unto you as unto spiritual, but as unto carnal, even as unto babes in Christ.

2 I have fed you with milk, and not with meat: for hitherto ye were not able to bear it, neither yet now are ye able.

3 For ye are yet carnal: for whereas there is among you envying, and strife, and divisions, are ye not carnal, and walk as men?

4 For while one saith, I am of Paul; and another, I am of Apollos; are ye not carnal?

5 Who then is Paul, and who is Apollos, but ministers by whom ye believed, even as the Lord gave to every man?

6 I have planted, Apollos watered; but God gave the increase.

7 So then neither is he that planteth any thing, neither he that watereth; but God that giveth the increase.

8 Now he that planteth and he that watereth are one: and every man shall receive his own reward according to his own labour.

9 For we are labourers together with God: ye are God's husbandry, ye are God's building.

10 According to the grace of God which is given unto me, as a wise masterbuilder, I have laid the foundation, and another buildeth thereon. But let every man take heed how he buildeth thereupon.

11 For other foundation can no man lay than that is laid, which is Jesus Christ.

21 Therefore let no man glory in men: for all things are yours;

22 Whether Paul, or Apollos, or Cephas, or the world, or life, or death, or things present, or things to come; all are yours;

23 And ye are Christ's; and Christ is God's.

No. 45. The Apostle's Method. *I Cor. 9. 18-27.*

18 What is my reward then? Verily that, when I preach the gospel, I may make the gospel of Christ without charge, and I abuse not my power in the gospel.

19 For though I be free from all men, yet have I made myself servant unto all, that I might gain the more.

20 And unto the Jews I became as a Jew, that I might gain the Jews; to them that are under the law, as under the law, that I might gain them that are under the law;

21 To them that are without law, as without law, (being not without law to God, but under the law to Christ,) that I might gain them that are without law.

22 To the weak became I as weak, that I might gain the weak: I am made all things

to all men, that I might by all means save some.

23 And this I do for the gospel's sake, that I might be partaker thereof with you.

24 Know ye not that they which run in a race run all, but one receiveth the prize? So run, that ye may obtain.

25 And every man that striveth for the mastery is temperate in all things. Now they do it to obtain a corruptible crown; but we an incorruptible.

26 I therefore so run, not as uncertainly; so fight I, not as one that beateth the air:

27 But I keep under my body, and bring it into subjection: lest that by any means, when I have preached to others, I myself should be a castaway

No. 46. Mutual Dependence. *I Cor. 12, 14-26.*

14 For the body is not one member, but many.

15 If the foot shall say, Because I am not the hand, I am not of the body; is it therefore not of the body?

16 And if the ear shall say, Because I am not the eye, I am not of the body; is it therefore not of the body?

17 If the whole body were an eye, where were the hearing? If the whole were hearing, where were the smelling?

18 But now hath God set the members every one of them in the body, as it hath pleased him.

19 And if they were all one member, where were the body?

20 But now are they many members, yet but one body.

21 And the eye cannot say unto the hand, I have no need of thee: nor again the head to the feet, I have no need of you.

22 Nay, much more those members of the

body, which seem to be more feeble, are necessary:

23 And those members of the body, which we think to be less honourable, upon these we bestow more abundant honour; and our uncomely parts have more abundant comeliness.

24 For our comely parts have no need: but God hath tempered the body together, having given more abundant honour to that part which lacked:

25 That there should be no schism in the body; but that the members should have the same care one for another.

26 And whether one member suffer, all the members suffer with it; or one member be honoured, all the members rejoice with it.

No. 47.   Liberal Giving. *II Cor. 9, 6–15.*

6 But this I say, He which soweth sparingly shall reap also sparingly; and he which soweth bountifully shall reap also bountifully.

7 Every man according as he purposeth in his heart, so let him give; not grudgingly, or of necessity: for God loveth a cheerful giver.

8 And God is able to make all grace abound toward you; that ye, always having all sufficiency in all things, may abound to every good work:

9 (As it is written, He hath dispersed abroad; he hath given to the poor: his righteousness remaineth for ever.

10 Now he that ministereth seed to the sower both minister bread for your food, and multiply your seed sown, and increase the fruits of your righteousness;)

11 Being enriched in every thing to all bountifulness, which causeth through us thanksgiving to God.

12 For the administration of this service not only supplieth the want of the saints, but is abundant also by many thanksgivings unto God;

13 While by the experiment of this ministration they glorify God for your professed subjection unto the gospel of Christ, and for your liberal distribution unto them, and unto all men;

14 And by their prayer for you, which long after you for the exceeding grace of God in you.

15 Thanks be unto God for his unspeakable gift.

No. 48.   Fruits of the Flesh and of the Spirit. *Gal. 5, 16–26.*

16 This I say then, Walk in the Spirit, and ye shall not fulfil the lust of the flesh.

17 For the flesh lusteth against the Spirit, and the Spirit against the flesh: and these are contrary the one to the other; so that ye cannot do the things that ye would.

18 But if ye be led of the Spirit, ye are not under the law.

19 Now the works of the flesh are manifest, which are these, Adultery, fornication, uncleanness, lasciviousness,

20 Idolatry, witchcraft, hatred, variance, emulations, wrath, strife, seditions, heresies,

21 Envyings, murders, drunkenness, revellings, and such like: of the which I tell you before, as I have also told you in time past, that they which do such things shall not inherit the kingdom of God.

22 But the fruit of the Spirit is love, joy, peace, longsuffering, gentleness, goodness, faith,

23 Meekness, temperance: against such there is no law.

24 And they that are Christ's have crucified the flesh with the affections and lusts.

25 If we live in the Spirit, let us also walk in the Spirit.

26 Let us not be desirous of vainglory, provoking one another, envying one another.

No. 49.   Helping One Another. *Gal. 6, 1–10.*

1 Brethren, if a man be overtaken in a fault, ye which are spiritual, restore such a one in the spirit of meekness; considering thyself, lest thou also be tempted.

2 Bear ye one another's burdens, and so fulfil the law of Christ.

3 For if a man think himself to be something, when he is nothing, he deceiveth himself.

4 But let every man prove his own work, and then shall he have rejoicing in himself alone, and not in another.

5 For every man shall bear his own burden.

6 Let him that is taught in the word communicate unto him that teacheth in all good things.

7 Be not deceived; God is not mocked: for whatsoever a man soweth, that shall he also reap.

8 For he that soweth to his flesh shall of the flesh reap corruption; but he that soweth to the Spirit shall of the Spirit reap life everlasting.

9 And let us not be weary in well doing: for in due season we shall reap, if we faint not.

10 As we have therefore opportunity, let us do good unto all men, especially unto them who are of the household of faith.

Songs.

No. 1. Sweet and Low.

ALFRED TENNYSON. JOSEPH BARNBY.

pp Larghetto.

1. Sweet and low, sweet and low, Wind of the west - ern sea, Low, low,
2. Sleep and rest, sleep and rest; Fa-ther will come to thee soon. Rest, rest on

sf p *mf*

breathe and blow, Wind of the west - ern sea. O - ver the roll - ing
moth - er's breast; Fa-ther will come to thee soon. Fa-ther will come to his
A. O - - ver the
Fa - - ther will

pp *p*

wa - ters go: Come from the dy - ing moon, and blow; Blow him a - gain to
babe in the nest, Sil - ver sails all out of the west; Un - der the sil - ver
wa - ters go, A.B. Come from the moon and blow,
come to his nest, Sil - ver sails out of the west;

f

Rall. e dim - in - u - en - - do.

Dim. *p*

me, While my lit - tle one, while my pret-ty one sleeps. . . . .
moon. Sleep, my lit - tle one; sleep, my pret-ty one, sleep. . . . .

No. 2.

Swanee River.

STEPHEN COLLINS FOSTER.

STEPHEN COLLINS FOSTER.

1. { Way down up-on the Swa-nee rib-ber, Far, far a-way,
   { All up and down de whole cre-a-tion, Sad-ly I roam,
2. { All round de lit-tle farm I wan-dered When I was young,
   { When I was play-ing with my brud-der, Hap-py was I,
3. { One lit-tle hut a-mong de bush-es, One dat I love,
   { When shall I hear de bees a-hum-ming All round de comb?

Dere's wha' my heart is turn-ing eb-ber, Dere's wha' de old folks stay.
Still long-ing for de old plan-ta-tion, And for de old folks at home.
Den ma-ny hap-py days I squandered, Ma-ny de songs I sung;
Oh! take me to my kind old mud-der, Dere let me live and die.
Still sad-ly to my mem'ry rush-es, No mat-ter where I rove.
When shall I hear de ban-jo tum-ming Down in my good old home?

CHORUS.

All de world am sad and drear-y, Eb-'ry-where I roam;

O, dark-ies, how my heart grows wea-ry, Far from de old folks at home.

No. 3.   There's Music in the Air.

Moderato.

1. There's mu-sic in the air When the in-fant morn is nigh, And faint its blush is
2. There's mu-sic in the air When the noontide's sul-try beam Re-flects a gold-en
3. There's mu-sic in the air When the twilight's gen-tle sigh Is lost on eve-ning's

CHORUS.   *2d. time pp.*

seen On the bright and laughing sky. Many a harp's ecstatic sound, With its thrill of
light On the distant mountain stream: When beneath some grateful shade, Sorrow's aching
breast, As its pensive beauties die. Then, O, then, the loved ones gone, Wake the pure ce-

joy profound, While we list en-chant-ed there, To the mu - sic in the air.
head is laid, Sweet-ly to the spir-it there, Comes the mu - sic in the air.
les-tial song, An - gel voic-es greet us there, In the mu - sic of the air.

No. 4.   Soft Music is Stealing.

MARY S. B. DANA.   GERMAN AIR.
Andante.

1. Soft, soft mu-sic is steal-ing, Sweet, sweet lingers the strain: Loud, loud now it is
2. Join, join, chil-dren of sad-ness, Send, send sor-row a - way; Now, now changing to
3. Sweet, sweet melody's numbers, Hark! hark! gently they swell, Deep, deep, waking from

Sweet Music is Stealing.

peal-ing, Waking the ech-oes a-gain. Yes, yes, yes, yes, Waking the ech-oes a-gain.
glad-ness, Warble a beau-ti-ful lay. Yes, yes, yes, yes, War-ble a beau-ti-ful lay.
slumbers Tho'ts in the bosom that dwell. Yes, yes, yes, yes, Tho'ts in the bosom that dwell.

No. 5.   Juanita.

mf

1. Soft o'er the fount-ain, Ling'ring falls the southern moon; Far o'er the mount-ain
2. When in thy dreaming, Moons like these shall shine again, And daylight beam-ing,

Breaks the day too soon! In thy dark eye's splendor, Where the warm light loves to dwell,
Prove thy dreams are vain, Wilt thou not, re-lent-ing, For thine ab-sent lov - er sigh,

p Slower.   *mf A tempo.*

Wea-ry looks, yet ten-der, Speak their fond farewell! Ni - ta! Jua - ni - ta!
In thy heart con-sent-ing To a pray'r gone by? Ni - ta! Jua - ni - ta!

Tenderly. Rit.

Ask thy soul if we should part! Ni - ta! Jua - ni - ta! Lean thou on my heart.
Let me lin - ger by thy side! Ni - ta! Jua - ni - ta! Be my own fair bride!

No. 6.   Columbia, the Gem of the Ocean.

D. T. SHAW.   D. T. SHAW.

Spirited.

1. O, Co-lum - bia, the gem of the o-cean, The home of the brave and the free,
2. When war winged its wide des-o - la-tion, And threatened the land to de-form,
3. The star-spangled banner bring hither, O'er Colum-bia's true sons let it wave;

The shrine of each pa-triot's de-vo-tion,   A world of-fers hom-age to thee.
The ark then of freedom's foun-da-tion,   Co-lum-bia, rode safe thro' the storm:
May the wreaths they have won never wither, Nor its stars cease to shine on the brave.

Thy mandates make heroes as-sem-ble,   When Lib-er-ty's form stands in view;
With the gar-lands of vic-t'ry a-round her, When so proud-ly she bore her brave crew,
May the serv - ice u - ni-ted ne'er sev-er,   But hold to their col-ors so true;

𝄆   FINE.

Thy banners make tyr-an - ny trem-ble,   When borne by the red, white and blue,
With her flag proud-ly floating be-fore her,   The boast of the red, white and blue,
The ar - my and na - vy for - ev - er,   Three cheers for the red, white and blue.

D. S.

When borne by the red, white and blue, When borne by the red, white and blue,   Thy
The boast of the red, white and blue,   The boast of the red, white and blue, With her
Three cheers for the red, white and blue, Three cheers for the red, white and blue,   The

Battle Hymn of the Republic.*

JULIA WARD HOWE.   MELODY: "JOHN BROWN'S BODY."

1. Mine eyes have seen the glo - ry of the com - ing of the Lord; He is
2. I have seen Him in the watch-fires of a hun-dred cir-cling camps; They have
3. I have read a fier - y gos - pel, writ in bur-nished rows of steel; "As ye
4. He has sound-ed forth the trum - pet that shall nev - er call re-treat; He is
5. In the beau - ty of the lil - ies, Christ was born a - cross the sea, With a

tramp-ling out the vin - tage where the grapes of wrath are stored; He hath
build - ed Him an al - tar in the ev-'ning dews and damps; I can
deal with my con-tem - ners, so with you my grace shall deal;" Let the
sift - ing out the hearts of men be - fore His judg-ment seat; O, be
glo - ry in His bo - som that trans - fig - ures you and me; As He

loosed the fate-ful lightning of His terrible swift sword. His truth is march-ing on.
read His righteous sentence by the dim and flaring lamps. His day is march-ing on.
He-ro, born of woman, crush the serpent with his heel, Since God is march-ing on.
swift, my soul, to an-swer Him! be ju - bi-lant my feet! Our God is march-ing on.
died to make men ho-ly, let us die to make men free, While God is march-ing on.

Glo-ry! glo-ry hal-le-lu-jah! Glo-ry! glo-ry hal-le-lu-jah!

{ His truth is marching on.
His day is marching on.
Since God is marching on.
Our God is marching on.
While God is marching on. }

* The words are used by permission of Houghton, Mifflin & Co.

No. 8.   The Star-Spangled Banner.

FRANCIS SCOTT KEY.

SOLO or QUARTET.

1. O,   say, can you see, by the dawn's early light, What so proudly we hailed at the
2. On the shore dimly seen thro' the mists of the deep, Where the foe's haughty host in dread
3. And where is that band who so vauntingly swore, That the hav-oc of war and the
4. O,   thus be it ev-er when freemen shall stand Be-tween their loved home and wild

twilight's last gleaming, Whose broad stripes and bright stars thro' the per-il-ous fight, O'er the
si-lence re-pos-es, What is that which the breeze, o'er the tow-er-ing steep, As it
bat-tle's con-fu-sion, A   home and a coun-try should leave us no more? Their
war's des-o-la-tion; Blest with vict'ry and peace, may the heav'n-rescued land Praise the

ramparts we watched, were so gallantly streaming? And the rocket's red glare, the bombs
fit-ful-ly blows, half conceals, half dis-clos-es? Now it catch-es the gleam   of the
blood has washed out their foul footsteps' pol-lu-tion. No   ref-uge could save   the
pow'r that hath made and pre-served us a   na-tion! Then con-quer we must, when our

CHORUS. *ff*

bursting in air, Gave proof thro' the night that our flag was still there. O, say, does that
morning's first beam, In full glo-ry re-flect-ed, now shines on the stream: 'Tis the star-spangled
hireling and slave From the terror of flight or the gloom of the grave: And the star-spangled
cause it is just, And this   be our mot-to: "In God is our trust!" And the star-spangled

The Star-Spangled Banner.

Cres.   ff

star-spangled ban-ner yet wave
ban-ner: O, long may it wave
ban-ner in triumph doth wave
ban-ner in triumph shall wave
O'er the land of the free and the home of the brave.

No. 9.   Decoration Day.

HENRY WADSWORTH LONGFELLOW.   JOHANN AEGIDIUS GEYER.

1. Sleep, com-rades, sleep, sleep and rest On this field of the
2. Rest, com-rades, rest, rest and sleep! The tho'ts of men shall
3. Your si-lent tents, tents of green, We deck with flow-ers, with

p

Ground-ed Arms, Where foes no more mo-lest, Nor sen-try's shot a-larms!
ev - er be As sen-ti-nels to keep Your rest from dan-ger free,
fra - grant flow'rs; Yours has the suf-f'ring been, The mem-'ry shall be ours,

Sleep, com-rades, sleep and rest On this Field of the Ground-ed Arms.
As sen-ti-nels to keep Your rest from dan-ger free.
Yours has the suf-f'ring been, The mem-'ry shall be ours.

No. 10.   Hail Columbia.

F. HOPKINSON.   F. HOPKINSON.

With energy.

1. Hail Co-lum-bia, hap-py land! Hail, ye he-roes, heav'n-born band,
2. Immor-tal pa-triots, rise once more, Defend your rights, de-fend your shore!
3. Behold the chief that now commands, Once more to serve his coun-try stands

Who fought and bled in free-dom's cause, Who fought and bled in freedom's cause,
Let no rude foe, with im-pious hand, Let no rude foe, with im-pious hand,
The rock on which the storm will beat, The rock on which the storm will beat,

And when the storm of war was gone En-joyed the peace your val-or won.
In-vade the shrine where sa-cred lies Of toil and blood the well-earned prize.
But armed in vir-tue, firm and true, His hopes are fixed on heav'n and you.

Let in-de-pen-dence be our boast, Ev-er mind-ful what it cost;
While of-f'ring peace, sin-cere and just, In heav'n we place a man-ly trust,
When hope was sink-ing in dis-may, When glooms obscured Columbia's day,

Ev-er grate-ful for the prize, Let its al-tar reach the skies.
That truth and jus-tice will pre-vail, And ev-'ry scheme of bond-age fail.
His stead-y mind, from chang-es free, Resolved on death or lib-er-ty.

Hail Columbia.

CHORUS.

Firm, u - ni - ted, let us be, Ral - ly - ing round our lib - er - ty,

As a band of broth-ers joined, Peace and safe - ty we shall find.

No. 11. Auld Lang Syne.

ROBERT BURNS.
p Slow.

1. Should auld acquaintance be for-got, And nev - er bro't to mind? Should auld ac-
2. We twa ha'e run a - boot the braes, And pu'd the gowans fine; But we've wandered
3. We twa ha'e sport-ed i' the burn Frae morn-in' sun till dine, But seas be-
4. And here's a hand, my trust - y frien', And gie's a hand o' thine; We'll tak' a

p CHORUS.

quaintance be for-got, And days of auld lang syne?
mony a wea-ry foot Sin' auld lang syne.
tween us braid ha'e roared Sin' auld lang syne. } For auld lang syne, my dear,
cup o' kind-ness yet, For auld lang syne.

Repeat Chorus ff

For auld lang syne; We'll tak' a cup o' kind-ness yet For auld lang syne.

No. 12.   Watch On the Rhine.

MAX SCHNECKENBURGER.   CARL WILHELM.

With energy.

1. A voice re-sounds like thun-der peal, 'Mid dash-ing wave and clang of steel;
2. They stand a hun-dred thou-sand strong, Quick to a - venge their country's wrong;
3. While flows one drop of Ger-man blood, Or sword re-mains to guard thy flood,
4. Our oath re-sounds, the riv - er flows, In gold - en light our ban-ner glows,

"The Rhine, the Rhine, the Ger-man Rhine! Who guards to-day my stream di-vine!"
With fil - ial love their bo - soms swell; They'll guard the sa-cred land-mark well.
While ri - fle rests in pa-triot's hand, No foe shall tread thy sa - cred strand!
Our hearts will guard thy stream di - vine, The Rhine, the Rhine, the Ger-man Rhine!

CHORUS.

Dear Fatherland! no danger thine, Dear Fa-ther-land! no danger thine; Firm stand thy

sons to watch, to watch the Rhine, Firm stand thy sons to watch, to watch the Rhine.

1 Es braust ein Ruf wie Donnerhall,
Wie Schwertgeklirr und Wogenprall:
Zum Rhein, zum Rhein, zum deutschen
Rhein!
Wer will des Stromes Hüter sein?

CHOR.

Lieb Vaterland, magst ruhig sein,
Lieb Vaterland, magst ruhig sein;
Fest steht und treu die Wacht, die Wacht
am Rhein!
Fest steht und treu die Wacht, die Wacht
am Rhein!

2 Durch Hunderttausend zuckt es schnell,
Und Aller Augen blitzen hell;
Der Deutsche, bieder, fromm und stark,
Beschützt die heil' ge Landesmark.

3 So lang' ein Tropfen Blut noch glüht,
Noch eine Faust den Degen zieht,
Und noch ein Arm die Büchse spannt,
Betritt kein Feind hier deinen Strand.

4 Der Schwur erschallt, die Woge rinnt,
Die Fahnen flattern hoch im Wind:
Am Rhein, am Rhein, am deutschen Rhein,
Wir alle wollen Hüter sein!

No. 13.   North German Cradle Song.

1. Sleep, ba - by, sleep! Thy fa-ther guards the sheep, Thy moth-er shakes the
2. Sleep, ba - by, sleep! The large stars are the sheep, The lit - tle ones the
3. Sleep, ba - by, sleep! Our Sav - ior loves His sheep, He is the Lamb of

Schlaf, Kind-chen, schlaf! Dein Va - ter hüt't die Schaf'; Deine Mut-ter schüt-telt's

dreamland tree, And from it fall sweet dreams for thee; Sleep, baby, sleep! Sleep, baby, sleep!
lambs, I guess, The gen-tle moon the shepherdess, Sleep, ba-by, sleep! Sleep, ba-by, sleep!
God on high, Who for our sakes came down to die, Sleep, ba-by, sleep! Sleep, ba-by, sleep!

Bäu-me-lein, Da fällt he-rab ein Träumelein; Schlaf, Kindchen, schlaf! Schlaf, Kindchen, schlaf!

No. 14.   Stars of the Summer Night.

LONGFELLOW.
p Andante.

ISAAC B. WOODBURY.
Poco cres.

1. Stars of the sum-mer night, Far in yon a - zure deeps, Hide, hide your
2. Moon of the sum-mer night, Far down yon west-ern steeps, Sink, sink in
3. Dreams of the sum-mer night, Tell her, her lov - er keeps Watch while, in

gold-en light, She sleeps, my la-dy sleeps, She sleeps, She sleeps, my la-dy sleeps.
sil-ver light, She sleeps, my la-dy sleeps, She sleeps, She sleeps, my la-dy sleeps.
slumbers light, She sleeps, my la-dy sleeps, She sleeps, She sleeps, my la-dy sleeps.

No. 15. Once I Saw a Rose.

H. WERNER.

H. WERNER.

Moderato.

1. Once I saw a sweet-brier rose, All so fresh-ly bloom-ing, Bathed with dew and
2. 'Rose," said I, "thou shalt be mine, All so fresh-ly bloom-ing;" Rose replied, "Nay,
3. Woe is me! I broke the stem, Life and fragrance doom-ing; Soon the love-ly
4. Had I left thee, love-ly flow'r, In thy beau-ty bloom-ing, Bathed with dew and

blush-ing fair, Gen - tly waved by balm - y air, All the air per-
let me go, Or thy blood shall free - ly flow For thy rash pre-
flow'r was gone, And the thorns re-mained a - lone— Van - ished all its
blush-ing fair, Thou wouldst still have filled the air With thy sweet per-

fum-ing: Gen - tly waved by balm-y air, All the air per - fum - ing.
sum-ing; Or thy blood shall free-ly flow For thy rash pre - sum - ing."
bloom-ing; And the thorns re-mained a - lone—Van-ished all its bloom - ing.
fum-ing; Thou wouldst still have filled the air, With thy sweet per - fum - ing.

No. 16. The Last Rose of Summer.

THOMAS MOORE.

1. 'Tis the last rose of sum-mer, Left bloom - ing a - lone; All her love-ly com-
2. I'll not leave thee, thou lone one, To pine on the stem, Since the love-ly are
3. So soon may I fol-low, When friend-ships de - cay, And from love's shining

The Last Rose of Summer.

pan-ions Are fad - ed and gone; No flow-er of her kin-dred, No
sleep-ing, Go sleep thou with them; Thus kind - ly I scat-ter Thy
cir - cle The gems drop a - way; When true hearts lie with-ered, And

rose - bud is nigh, To re-flect back her blushes, Or give sigh for sigh.
leaves o'er the bed, Where thy mates of the gar-den Lie scent-less and dead.
fond ones are flown, O, who would in - hab-it This bleak world a - lone!

No. 17.   Forsaken.*

KOSCHAT.

Lento.

pp

mf

pp

1. For-sak - en, for - sak-en, for-sak - en am I: Like a stone in the cause-way, my
2. A mound in the church-yard, that blossoms hang o'er; It is there my love sleepeth, to

Cres.

bur-ied hopes lie; I go to the churchyard, my eyes fill with tears; And kneeling I
wak-en no more; 'Tis there all my foot-steps, my passions all lead; And there my heart

ff   p   Cres.   ff   p

weep there. O, my love, loved for years; And kneel-ing I weep there; O, my love, loved for years.
turn-eth; I'm for-sak - en in-deed; And there my heart turneth; I'm for-sak-en in - deed.

* It will be well to strengthen the tenor part by the addition of a few low alto voices.

No. 18. Farewell to the Forest.

MENDELSSOHN.

p Andante.

1. Thou for-est broad and sweeping, Fair work of na-ture's God, Of all my joy and
2. Who right-ly scans thy beau - ty, A sol-emn word shall read Of love, of truth and
3. Ah! soon must I for-sake thee, My own, my shelt'ring home, In sor-row soon be-

weep - ing, The con - se-crate a-bode! Yon world de-ceiv-ing ev - er,
du - ty, Our hope in time of need. And I have read them oft - en,
take me, In yon vain world to roam. And there the word re - call - ing,

Yon world de - ceiv - ing ev - er,
And I have read them oft - en,
And there the word re - call - ing,

Cres.

Yon world de - ceiv - ing ev - er,
And I have read them oft-en,
And there the word re-call-ing,

f *pp*

Mur-murs in vain a - larms, O, might I wan-der nev - er From thy pro-tect-ing
Those words so true and clear, What heart that would not soft-en, Thy wis-dom to re-
Thy sol-emn les-sons teach, 'Mid care and dan-ger fall - ing, No harm my soul shall

O, might I wan - der nev - er, O,
What heart that would not soft - en, What
'Mid care and dan - ger fall - ing, 'Mid

From thy pro - tect - ing arms!
Thy wis - dom to re - vere?
No harm my soul shall reach.

f *Dim.* *p*

arms! O, might I wan-der nev - er, From thy pro-tect-ing arms!
vere, What heart that would not soft - en Thy wis - dom to re - vere?
reach, 'Mid care and dan-ger fall - ing, No harm my soul shall reach.

might I wan-der nev - er, From thy pro - tect - ing arms!
heart that would not soft - en, Thy wis - dom to re - vere?
care and dan-ger fall - ing, No harm my soul shall reach.

No. 19. Rocked in the Cradle of the Deep.

1. Rocked in the cra-dle of the deep, I lay me down in peace to sleep;
2. And such the trust that still were mine, Tho' storm-y winds sweep o'er the brine,

Se-cure I rest up-on the wave, For Thou, O Lord, hast pow'r to save.
Or tho' the tem-pest's fier-y breath Roused me from sleep to wreck and death.

I know Thou wilt not slight my call, For Thou dost mark the spar-row's fall!
In o-cean wave still safe with Thee, The gem of im-mor-tal-i-ty;

And calm and peace-ful is my sleep, Rocked in the cra-dle of the deep,

And calm and peace-ful is my sleep, Rocked in the cra-dle of the deep.

No. 20. The Loreley.

HEINE.

F. SILCHER.

1. O, tell me what it meaneth, This gloom and tear-ful eye? 'Tis mem-'ry that re-
2. A-bove the maid-en sit-teth, A won-drous form and fair; With jew-els bright she
3. The boat-man on the riv-er Lists to the song, spell-bound; O, what shall him de-

tain-eth The tale of years gone by; The fad-ing light grows dim-mer, The
plait-eth Her shin-ing gold-en hair: With comb of gold pre-pares it, The
liv-er From dan-ger threat'ning round? The wa-ters deep have caught them, Both

Rhine doth calm-ly flow! The loft-y hill-tops glim-mer Red with the sun-set glow.
task with song be-guiled; A fit-ful bur-den bears it—That mel-o-dy so wild.
boat and boat-men brave; 'Tis Loreley's song hath bro't them Beneath the foaming wave.

No. 21. Speed Away!

ISAAC B. WOODBURY.

ISAAC B. WOODBURY.

pp Tenderly. *p*   *mp*

1. Speed a-way! speed a-way! on thine er-rand of light! There's a young heart a-
2. And O, wilt thou tell her, blest bird on the wing, That her moth-er hath
3. Go, bird of the sil-ver wing! fet-ter-less now; Stop not thy bright

mf

wait-ing thy com-ing to-night; She will fon-dle thee close, she will ask for the
ev-er a sad song to sing; That she stand-eth a-lone, in the still qui-et
pin-ions on yon mountain's brow; But hie thee a-way, o'er rock, riv-er and

Speed Away!

loved, Who pine up-on earth since the "Day Star" has roved, She will ask if we
night, And her fond heart goes forth for the be-ing of light, Who had slept in her
glen, And find our young "Day Star," ere night close a-gain; Up, on-ward! let

pp   *mf*   *Rit. e dim.*   *pp*

miss her, so long is her stay. }
bo-som,—but who would not stay? } Speed a-way! Speed a-way! Speed a - way!
noth-ing thy mis-sion de - lay. }

No. 22.   ## Murmur, Gentle Lyre.   ARR. BY E. O. LYTE.

1. Mur-mur, gen-tle lyre,   Thro' the lone - ly night;   Let thy trembling
2. Hark! the quiv'ring breez-es   List thy sil - v'ry sound;   Ev-'ry tu-mult
3. Earth be - low is sleep-ing,   Mead-ow, hill and grove;   An-gel stars are

wire   Wak - en dear de - light!   Tho' the tones of sor - row
ceas - es,   Si - lence reigns pro - found.   Hushed the thou-sand nois - es,
keep-ing   Si - lent watch a - bove.   Mur-mur, gen - tle lyre,

Min-gle in thy strain,   Yet my heart can bor-row Pleas-ure from the pain.
Gone the noon-day glare,   Gen-tle spir-it voic - es Ech - o thro' the air.
Thro' the lone-ly night;   Let thy trembling wire Wak - en deep de - light.

No. 23. Have Courage, my Boy, to Say No!

H. R. PALMER.

1. You're start-ing, my boy, on your jour-ney, A - long the grand high-way of life;
2. In cour-age a - lone lies your safe - ty, When you the long jour-ney be - gin;
3. Be care-ful in choos-ing com-pan-ions, Seek on - ly the brave and the true;

You'll meet with a thou-sand temptations—Each cit-y with e - vil is rife.
Your trust in a heav - en-ly Fa - ther, Will keep you up-spot-ted from sin.
And stand by your friends when in tri - al, Ne'er changing the old for the new;

This world is a stage of ex-cite-ment, There's dan-ger wher-ev-er you go;
Temp-ta-tions will go on in - creas-ing, As streams from a riv-u - let flow;
And when by false friends you are tempted The taste of the wine-cup to know;

But if you are tempt-ed in weak-ness, Have courage, my boy, to say No!
But if you'd be true to your man-hood, Have courage, my boy, to say No!
With firmness, with patience and kindness, Have courage, my boy, to say No!

CHORUS.

Have courage, my boy, to say No! Have courage, my boy, to say No!

say no!   say no!

Copyright, 1887, by H. R. Palmer.

Have Courage, my Boy, to Say No!

Have courage, my boy, Have courage, my boy, Have courage, my boy, to say No!

No. 24.   Annie Laurie.

1. Max-wel-ton's banks are bonnie, Where ear-ly fa's the dew, And 'twas there that An-nie
2. Her brow is like the snaw-drift, Her throat is like the swan; Her   face it is the
3. Like dew on th' gowan ly - ing Is th' fa' o' her fair-y feet, And like winds in Sum-mer

Cres.

Lau-rie Gave me her prom-ise true, Gave me her prom-ise true, Which ne'er forgot will
fair-est That e'er the sun shone on, That e'er the sun shone on,   And dark blue is her
sigh-ing, Her voice is   low and sweet, Her voice is low and sweet, And she's a' the world to

be,   And for bon-nie An - nie Lau - rie, I'd lay me down and dee.
e'e, And for bon-nie An - nie Lau - rie, I'd lay me down and dee.
me   And for bon-nie An - nie Lau - rie, I'd lay me down and dee.

No. 25. The Old Oaken Bucket.

SAMUEL WOODWORTH.

1. How dear to this heart are the scenes of my child-hood, When fond rec - ol-
2. That moss-cov-ered buck - et I hailed as a treas - ure, For oft - en at
3. How sweet from the green moss-y brim to re - ceive it, As, poised on the

lec-tion pre-sents them to view! The or-chard, the mead-ow, the deep-tan-gled
noon, when returned from the field, I found it a source of an ex - quis - ite
curb, it in-clined to my lips! Not a full-blush-ing gob - let could tempt me to

wild-wood, And ev - 'ry loved spot which my in - fan - cy knew, The wide-spread-ing
pleas-ure, The pur - est and sweetest that na - ture can yield. How ar - dent I
leave it, Tho' filled with the nec-tar that Ju - pi - ter sips. And now, far re-

pond, and the mill that stood by it, The bridge and the rock where the
seized it, with hands that were glow - ing, And quick to the white - peb-bled
moved from the loved hab - i - ta - tion, The tear of re - gret will in-

cat - a - ract fell. The cot of my fa - ther, the dai - ry-house nigh it, And
bot-tom it fell. Then soon, with the em-blem of truth o - ver - flow-ing, And
tru-sive - ly swell, As fan - cy re - verts to my fa-ther's plan - ta-tion, And

The Old Oaken Bucket

e'en the rude buck-et that hung in the well. The old oak-en buck-et, the
drip-ping with cool-ness, it rose from the well. The old oak-en buck-et, the
sighs for the buck-et that hung in the well. The old oak-en buck-et, the

i - ron-bound buck-et, The moss-cov-ered buck-et that hung in the well.
i - ron-bound buck-et, The moss-cov-ered buck-et a - rose from the well.
i - ron-bound buck-et, The moss-cov-ered buck-et which hangs in the well.

No. 26. Soldier's Farewell.

JOHANNA KINKEL.

p Andante. *p Poco riten.*

1. How can I bear to leave thee? One part-ing kiss I give thee; And
2. Ne'er more may I be-hold thee, Or to this heart en - fold thee; With
3. I think of thee with long-ing, Think thou, when tears are throng-ing, That

Crescendo e poco accel. al f.

then what-e'er be - falls me, I go where hon - or calls me, Fare-
spear and pen - non glanc-ing, I see the foe ad - vanc-ing, Fare-
with my last faint sigh -ing, I'll whis - per soft, while dy -ing, Fare-

Tempo I. Tranquillo e molto espress. f fz p pp

well, fare-well, my own true love, Fare-well, fare-well, my own true love.

No. 27.   Robin Adair.

CAROLINE KEPPEL.
Expression.

CAROLINE KEPPEL.

1. What's this dull town to me? Rob - in's not near. What was't I wished to see,
2. What made th'assembly shine? Rob-in A - dair. What made the ball so fine?
3. But now thou'rt cold to me, Rob - in A - dair. But now thou'rt cold to me,

What wished to hear? Where's all the joy and mirth, That made this town a
Rob - in was there; What, when the play was o'er, What made my
Rob - in A - dair, Yet him I loved so well, Still in my

heav'n on earth? O, they're all fled with thee, Rob - in A - dair.
heart so sore? O, it was part - ing with Rob - in A - dair.
heart shall dwell; O, I can ne'er for - get Rob - in A - dair.

No. 28.   O Come, Come Away.

W. E. HICKSON.

W. E. HICKSON.

Allegro.

1. O come, come a - way, From la - bor now re - pos - ing, Let bu - sy care a-
2. From toil and from care, On which the day is clos - ing, The hour of eve brings
3. While sweet Phil-o-mel, The wea-ry trav-'ler cheer-ing, With ev -'ning song her
4. The bright day is gone, The moon and stars ap-pear - ing, With sil - v'ry light il-

O, Come, Come Away.

while for-bear, O come, come a - way. Come, come, our so-cial joys re-new, And
sweet reprieve, O come, come a - way. O, come where love will smile on thee, And
notes pro-long, O come, come a - way. In an-sw'ring song of sym - pa - thy, We'll
lume the night, O come, come a - way. We'll join in grate-ful songs of praise, To

there with trust and friendship, too, Let true hearts welcome you, O come, come a-way.
round the heart will gladness be, And time fly mer - ri - ly, O come, come a-way.
sing in tune-ful har - mo-ny, Of hope, joy, lib - er - ty, O come, come a-way.
Him who crowns our peaceful day With health, hope, happiness, O come, come a-way.

No. 29.   On Alpine Heights.

GERSBACH.

1. On Al-pine heights There dwells a God of love; The morn-ing's ros-y
2. On Al-pine heights, There, 'mid the clouds of snow, From grass-y slopes be-

hue, He paints and bathes in dew The flow-'rets white and blue;
low, The spi - cy zeph - yrs bear A fra-grance pure and clear;

On Al - pine heights There dwells a God of love.

Help it On.

E. R. SILL.   OLD MELODY.

1. There's a good time com-ing, Help it on,   There's a good time
2. There's a fu-ture on the way, Help it on, There's a fu-ture on the
3. When you find a no-ble cause, Help it on, When you find a no-ble
4. When the right shall win, Help it on,   When the right shall
                                   Help it on,

com-ing, Help it on,   Ev-'ry heart its tune is drumming, All the
way, Help it on,   When the night shall turn to-day   For the
cause, Help it on,   Nev-er wait for man's ap-plause, Nev-er
win, Help it on,   There will be no want nor sin,   And the
        Help it on,

air with it is humming, Help it on, Help it on, Help it on, on, on!
right shall have the way, Help it on, Help it on, Help it on, on, on!
count the cost or pause, Help it on, Help it on, Help it on, on, on!
good time shall be-gin, Help it on, Help it on, Help it on, on, on!

No. 31.   Blue Bells of Scotland.

1. O where and O where is your High-land lad-die gone?
2. O where and O where did your High-land lad-die dwell?
3. Sup-pose and sup-pose that your High-land lad should die?

Blue Bells of Scotland.

He's gone to fight the French, for King George up - on the throne—
He dwelt in mer - ry Scot - land, At sign of the Blue Bell—
The bag-pipes should play o'er him, And I'd sit down and cry—

And it's O in my heart, I wish him safe at home.
And it's O in my heart, I love my lad - die well.
But it's O in my heart, I hope he may not die.

No. 32.   Good-Night.

f Sostenuto.

1. Good-night, la - dies! good-night, la - dies! Good-night, la - dies!
2. Fare - well, la - dies! fare - well, la - dies! Fare - well, la - dies!
3. Sweet dreams, la - dies! sweet dreams, la - dies! Sweet dreams, la - dies!

Allegro.

We're going to leave you now. Mer - ri-ly we roll a - long, roll a - long,

roll a - long, Mer - ri - ly we roll a - long, O'er the dark blue sea.

No. 33.   **Flow Gently, Sweet Afton.**

ROBERT BURNS.   J. E. SPILMAN.

1. Flow gen-tly, sweet Af-ton, amang thy green braes; Flow gently, I'll sing thee a
2. How loft - y, sweet Af-ton, thy neighboring hills, Far mark'd with the courses of
3. Thy crystal stream, Af-ton, how love-ly it glides, And winds by the cot where my

song in thy praise; My Ma-ry's a-sleep by thy murmuring stream, Flow gently, sweet
clear-winding rills; There dai-ly I wan-der, as morn ris - es high, My flocks and my
Ma - ry re-sides! How wan-ton thy wa-ters her snow-y feet lave, As gath'ring sweet

Af - ton, dis-turb not her dream. Thou stock-dove, whose echo re-sounds from the
Ma-ry's sweet cot in my eye. How pleasant thy banks and green val-leys be-
flowerets, she stems thy clear wave! Flow gently, sweet Af-ton, a-mang thy green

Cres.

hill, Ye wild whistling black-birds in yon thorn-y dell, Thou green-crested
low, Where wild in the woodlands the prim-ros - es blow! There oft, as mild
braes, Flow gen - tly, sweet riv - er, the theme of my lays: My Ma - ry's a -

lap-wing, thy screaming for-bear, I charge you, disturb not my slum-ber-ing fair.
evening creeps o - ver the lea, The sweet-scented birk shades my Mary and me.
sleep by thy mur-mur-ing stream, Flow gently, sweet Af-ton, dis-turb not her dream.

Hail to the Queen of Night.

GERMAN.

Maestoso.

1. Hail to the Queen of the si - lent night, Shine clear, shine bright, Yield thy pensive light;
2. Dart thy pure beams from thy throne on high, Beam on, thro' sky, Rob'd in a - zure dye;

Blith - ly we'll dance in thy sil - ver ray, Hap - pi - ly pass - ing the
We'll laugh and we'll sport while the night-bird sings, Flapping the dew from his

hours a - way. Must we not love the still - y night, Dress'd in her robes of
sa - ble wings: Sprites love to sport in the still moon-light, Play with the pearls of

blue and white? Heav'n's arches ring, Stars wink and sing, Hail, si - lent night!
shad-owy night: Then let us sing, Time's on the wing, Hail, si - lent night!

Fair-y moon-light, fair-y moon-light, fair-y moon - - - light.
fair-y, fair-y, fair-y moonlight.

No. 35. Rain on the Roof.

COL. COATES KINNEY.

ISAAC B. WOODBURY

1. When the hu - mid show-ers gath - er O - ver all the star - ry spheres,
2. Ev - 'ry tin - kle on the shingles Has an ech - o in the heart,
3. There is naught in art's bra - vu - ras That can work with such a spell,

La la la la la la la la la la la la la la la la la

And the mel - an - chol-y dark-ness Gen-tly weeps in rain - y tears, 'Tis a
And a thousand dream-y fan - cies In - to bus - y be-ings start; And a
In the spir-it's pure, deep fountains, Whence the ho-ly pass-ions swell, As that

la la la la la la la la la la la la la la.

Cres.

joy to press the pil - low Of a cot - age-cham-ber bed, And to
thou-sand rec - ol - lec - tions Weave their bright hues in - to woof, As I
mel - o - dy of na - ture, That sub-dued, sub - du - ing strain, Which is

lis - ten to the pat - ter Of the soft rain o - ver - head.. La la
lis - ten to the pat - ter Of the soft rain on the roof.
play'd up - on the shin - gles By the pat - ter of the rain.

La la la la la la,

la la la la la la la la la la la la la................
la la la la la la la la la la la la la la la.

Home, Sweet Home.

JOHN HOWARD PAYNE.

1. Mid pleasures and pal - a - ces, though we may roam, Be it ev - er so
2. An ex - ile from home, splendor daz-zles in vain; O! give me my

humble, there's no place like home; A charm from the skies seems to hal-low us
low - ly thatched cottage a-gain,—The birds sing-ing gai - ly, that came at my

Cres.

there, Which, seek thro' the world, is ne'er met with else-where. Home!
call; Give me them, with the peace of mind, dear - er than all.

Rit. *Cres.*

home! sweet, sweet home! Be it ev - er so hum-ble, there's no place like home.

No. 37.

Row Your Boat.

E. O. LYTE.

1. (Round.) 2.

Row, row, row your boat, Gen - tly down the stream;

3. 4.

Mer - ri - ly, mer-ri - ly, mer - ri - ly, mer-ri - ly; Life is but a dream.

No. 38. Love's Old Sweet Song.

G. F. BRIGHAM.   J. L. MOLLOY.

1. Once in the dear, dead days be-yond re - call,   When on the world the
2. E - ven to - day we hear love's song of yore,   Deep in our hearts it

mists be - gan to fall,   Out of the dreams that rose in hap-py throng,
dwells for ev - er more;   Foot-steps may fal - ter, wea - ry grow the way,

Low to. our hearts love sang an old sweet song;   And in the dusk, where
Still we can hear it at the close of day.   So to the end, when

Love's Old Sweet Song.

fell the twilight gleam, Soft-ly it wove it-self in-to our dream.
life's dim shadows fall, Love will be found the sweetest song of all.

Rit.

CHORUS.

Just a song at twi-light, when the lights are low,
the lights are low,

And the flick-'ring shad-ows soft-ly come and go,
soft-ly go,

Tho' the heart be wea-ry, sad the day and long, Still to us at
the day is long,

twi-light, comes love's old song, Comes love's old sweet song.

No. 39.   The Little Brown Church.

W. S. P.

WM. S. PITTS.

1. There's a church in the valley by the wild-wood, No love-li-er place in the dale,
2. How sweet on a bright Sabbath morn-ing, To list to the clear-ring-ing bell,
3. There close by the church in the val - ley, Lies one that I lov - ed so well;

No spot is so dear to my child-hood, As the little brown church in the vale.
Its tones so sweet-ly are call - ing, O, come to the church in the vale.
She sleeps, sweetly sleeps 'neath the willow, Dis - turb not her rest in the vale.

CHORUS.

Come to the church by the wild - wood,

O, come, come, come, come, come, come, come, come, come, come, come,

O, come to the church in the vale,

come, come, come, come, come, come, come, come, No spot is so

dear to my child - hood, As the lit - tle brown church in the vale.

No. 40.   Marseilles Hymn.

ROUGET DE LISLE.

1. Ye sons of France, awake to glo - ry! Hark, hark! what myriads bid you rise!
2. With lux - u - ry and pride sur - round - ed, The vile, in - sa - tiate des pots dare,
3. O Lib - er - ty! can man re - sign thee, Once having felt thy gen - rous flame?

Your children, wives, and grand-sires hoar-y: Behold their tears, and hear their cries,
Their thirst for gold and pow'r un-bound - ed, To mete and vend the light and air,
Can dungeons, bolts and bars con - fine thee? Or whips thy no - ble spir - it tame?

Be-hold their tears and hear their cries! Shall hateful ty-rants mis-chief breed-ing,
To mete and vend the light and air. Like beasts of bur-den would they load us,
Or whips thy no - ble spir - it tame? Too long the world has wept be - wail-ing

With hire-ling hosts, a ruf - fian band, Af-fright and des-o-late the land, While
Like gods would bid their slaves adore; But man is man, and who is more? Then
That falsehood's dagger ty-rants wield; But freedom is our sword and shield, And

peace and lib-er-ty lie bleeding!
shall they longer lash and goad us? } To arms, to arms, ye brave! Th'avenging sword un-
all their arts are un-a-vail-ing:

Marseilles Hymn.

sheathe ! March on, march on, all hearts re-solved On. vic - to-ry or death !

No. 41. When the Swallows Homeward Fly.

FRANZ ABT.

1. When the swal-lows homeward fly, When the ros - es scat-tered lie, When from
2. When the white swan southward roves, To seek at noon the orange groves, When the
3. Hush, my heart! why thus complain? Thou must, too, thy woes con-tain, Tho' on

nei - ther hill nor dale, Chants the sil - v'ry night-in-gale ; In these words my bleeding
red tints of the west Prove the sun has gone to rest; In these words my bleeding
earth no more we rove, Loud-ly breathing words of love; Thou, my heart, must find re-

heart Would to thee its grief im - part, When I thus thy im - age lose,
heart Would to thee its grief im - part, When I thus thy im - age lose,
lief, Yield-ing to these words be - lief; I shall see thy form a - gain,

Can I, ah, can I e'er know re-pose, Can I, ah, can I e'er know re-pose?
Can I, ah, can I e'er know re-pose, Can I, ah, can I e'er know re-pose?
Tho' to - day we part a - gain, Tho' to - day we part a - gain.

No. 42.   The Wayside Cross.

THE LOST LANDMARK.

MRS. CORNIE LAWS ST. JOHN.   H. R. PALMER.

SOLO. *May be sung by a smooth bass voice.*

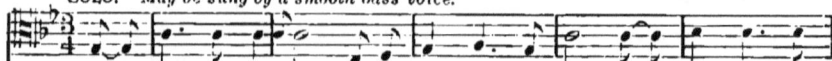

1. "Which way shall I take?" shouts a voice on the night, "I'm a pil-grim a-
2. "Which way shall I take for the bright gold-en span That bridg-es the
3. "See the lights from the palace in sil-ver-y lines, How they pen-cil the

wea-ried, and spent is my light; And I seek for the palace that
wa-ters so safe-ly for man? To the right? to the left? ah
hedg-es and fruit-la-den vines— My fortune! my all for

Rit.

rests on the hill, But be-tween us, a stream li-eth, sul-len and chill.
me! if I knew—The night is so dark, and the pass-ers so few.
one tan-gled gleam That sifts thro' the lil-ies, and wastes on the stream."

p   *Rit.*

Copyright, 1884, by H. R. Palmer.

The Wayside Cross.

CHORUS.
1ST AND 2D TENOR. *May be sung by ladies in tenor voice, tenors singing the baritone.*

Near, near thee, my son, is the old way-side cross, Like a gray fri - ar cowled, in

BARITONE.

BASS.

lichens and moss; And its cross-beam will point to the bright golden span, That bridges the

waters so safe-ly for man. That bridges the waters so safe-ly for man.

CODA. *pp to be sung after last stanza.*

wa-ters so safe-ly for man. That bridges the waters so safe-ly for man.

No. 43. Pastorale.

Gently.

GLUCK.

1. { O sweet, O sweet, when first the sun Comes laughing out his course to run: }
   { When night so drear and dawn so gray Blush o'er with joy to yield him way: }
2. { O sweet, O sweet, when first the sun His day-long course has spent and run: }
   { When cottage roofs with smoke are crown'd, When stars are blink-ing out a-round: }
3. { O sweet, O sweet, who's life's first morn The smiles of blame-less mirth a-dorn: }
   { Whose widening years with joy are fraught From wisdom's own clear sunshine caught: }

When larks mount high and lin-nets sing, And all things give their wel-com-ing.
When birds with song re-seek their nest, And all things fold them-selves to rest.
Who sleep be - neath the pure de-fence, Life wins in age from in - no-cence.

No. 44. My Old Kentucky Home.

STEPHEN COLLINS FOSTER.

Rather slow.

1. The sun shines bright in the old Kentucky home, 'Tis summer, the darkies are gay;
2. They hunt no more for the possum and the coon, On the meadow, the hill, and the shore,
3. The head must bow and the back will have to bend, Wher-ev-er the darkey may go;

1st verse.

The corn top's ripe and the meadow's in the bloom, While the birds make music all the
They sing no more by the glimmer of the moon, On the
A few more days, and the troub-le all will end In the

2nd verse. *3rd verse.*

bench by the old cab-in
field where the su-gar-canes grow; A few more days for to

day. The young folks roll on the
door. The day goes by like a

lit-tle cab-in floor, All merry, all happy and bright, By'm-by hard times comes a knocking at the door,
shadow o'er the heart, With sorrow where all was delight; The time has come when the darkies have to part,
tote the weary load, No matter, 'twill never be light, A few more days till we totter on the road,

CHORUS.

Then, my old Kentucky home, good night! Weep no more, my la-dy, Oh! weep no more to-day!

My Old Kentucky Home.

We will sing one song for the old Kentucky home, For the old Kentucky home, far a-way.

No. 45.

Bonnie Doon.

1. Ye banks and braes of bon-nie Doon, How can ye bloom sae fresh and fair, How
2. Oft have I strayed by bon-nie Doon, To see the rose and woodbine twine; Where

can ye sing, ye lit - tle birds, And I sae wea-ry, full of care? You'll
il - ka bird sang of his love, And fond-ly sae did I o' mine, With

break my heart, ye lit - tle birds, That wan-ton thro' the flow'ring thorn; Ye
light-some heart I pulled a rose, Full sweet up - on its thorn-y tree; But

mind me of de - part - ed joys, De - part-ed, nev - er to re - turn.
my false lov - er stole the rose, And left the thorn be - hind to me.

Glo - ry and love to the men of old, Their sons may

cop - y their vir-tues bold, Cour - age in heart and a sword in hand, Yes,

read - y to fight or read - y to die for Fa - ther - land.

Who needs bid - ding to dare by a trum - pet blown?

Who lacks pit-y to spare, when the field is won? Who would fly from a foe,

Soldiers' Chorus.

.... if a - lone or last? And boast he was true, as cow-ard might do, when

per - il is past? Glo - ry and love to the men of old,

Their sons may cop - y their vir - tues bold. Cour - age in

heart, and a sword in hand, Read - y to fight for Fa - ther - land.

Now..... home a - gain, we come, the long and fier - y strife of bat - tle

Soldiers' Chorus.

o - ver.   Rest is pleas-ant af - ter toil, as hard as ours be -

neath a stran-ger sun.   Ma-ny a maid-en fair is wait-ing

here to greet her tru-ant sol-dier lov - er,   And many a heart will fail, and

brow grow pale to hear the tale of per-il he has seen.   We are at

D. C.

home,   we are at home, we are at home, we are at home.

No. 47.
Vale.
(ETON SONG, adapted.)

A. C. AINGER.

J. BARNBY.

Allegretto.

mp

1. Time ev - er flow-ing bids us be go - ing, Moth-er A - del -phi, far from thee,
2. Life's du-ties call us; what-e'er be-fall us, High lot or low - ly, weal or woe,
3. A - del-phi fa - ces, A - del-phi pla - ces, Tho' we be part - ed far a - way,

Hearts growing old - er, love nev-er cold - er, Nev - er for-got-ten shalt thou be.
Broth-er with brother, thou our dear mother, In thee u - nit - ed we will go.
Seen ev - er clear-ly, lov'd ev - er dear-ly, Shall then be with us as to - day;

No. 48.
Flag of the Free.

MARCH FROM "LOHENGRIN."

1. Flag of the free, fair - est to see! Borne thro' the strife and the thunder of war;
2. Flag of the brave, long may it wave, Chos - en of God while His might we adore, In

FINE.

Ban-ner so bright with star - ry light, Float ev - er proud-ly from mountain to shore.
Lib - er-ty's van for manhood of man, Sym-bol of Right thro' the years passing o'er.

D.S.—*While thro'the sky loud rings the cry,   U-nion and Lib - er - ty! one ev-er-more!*

D. S.

Emblem of freedom, hope to the slave, Spread thy fair folds but to shield and to save,
Pride of our country, honored a - far, Scatter each cloud that would darken a star,

Index of Authors of Hymns.

[NOTE.—Some acquaintance with the lives of noted hymn writers and with the circumstances under which their best hymns were written is of value, especially to students. The lives and works of the great composers of sacred music may also be studied with much interest and profit. Such studies as these will give new meaning and added interest to many a hymn and tune.

Among the most helpful aids in hymn studies are the following: Charles S. Robinson's Annotations Upon Popular Hymns; Methodist Book Concern, N. Y., $2.50. Samuel W. Duffield's English Hymns; Funk & Wagnall's, N. Y., $2.50. Charles S. Nutter's Hymn Studies; Methodist Book Concern, N. Y., $1 90.]

ADAMS, MRS. SARA FLOWER, 1805-1849, English, No. 65.
ADDISON, JOSEPH, 1672-1719, English, Nos. 10, 134.
AUBER, HARRIET, 1773-1862, English, No. 16.
BAKEWELL, REV. JOHN, 1721-1819, English, No. 19.
BARBAULD, MRS. ANNA L., 1743-1825, English, No. 34.
BARING-GOULD, REV. SABINE, 1834-   , English, Nos. 45, 74.
BERNARD OF CLAIRVAUX, 1091-1153, French, Nos. 29, 69.
BERNARD OF CLUNY, 1122 (?)-   , French, No. 122.
BETHUNE, REV. GEO. W., 1805-1862, American, No. 19.
BONAR, REV. HORATIUS, D.D., 1808-1889, Scotch, Nos. 66, 95, 102, 108.
BONAR, MRS. CATHERINE,   -1885, Scotch, No. 92.
BOWRING, SIR JOHN, 1792-1872, English, No. 4.
CAWOOD, REV. JOHN, 1775-1852, English, No. 24.
CENNICK, REV. JOHN, 1717-1755, English, Nos. 70, 71.
COX, CHRISTOPHER C., M.D., 1816-   , No. 146.
CROSBY, FANNY, (Mrs. Alex. Van Alstyne), 1823-   , American, No. 83.
DOANE, BISHOP GEO. W., 1799-1859, American, No. 9.
DODDRIDGE, REV. PHILIP, D.D., 1702-1751, English, Nos. 7, 41, 103, 136.
DUFFIELD, REV. GEORGE, D.D., 1818-1888, American, No. 89.
DWIGHT, REV. TIMOTHY, D.D., 1752-1817, American, No. 13.
ELLERTON, REV. JOHN, 1826-   , English, No. 97.
ELLIOTT, MISS CHARLOTTE, 1789-1871, English, Nos. 49, 120, 141.
ESLING, MRS. CATHERINE H., No. 63.
FABER, REV. FREDERICK W., D.D., 1814-1863, English, Nos. 44, 51, 72, 141, 148.
FAWCETT, REV. JOHN, D.D., 1739-1817, English, Nos. 28, 106.
GERHARDT, REV. PAUL, 1606-1676, German, No. 30.
HARBAUGH, REV. HENRY, 1818-1867, American, No. 114.
HAWEIS, REV. HUGH R., 1838-   , English, No. 145.
HEATH, REV. GEORGE (Date of Hymn 1781), English, No. 80.
HIGBEE, REV. E. E., D.D., 1830-1889, American, No. 109.
HEBER, REV. BISHOP REGINALD, 1783-1826, English, Nos. 3, 52, 73, 142.
HOPPER, REV. EDWARD, D.D., 1818-1888, American, No. 100.
KEBLE, REV. JOHN, 1792-1866, English, No. 8.
KEITH, GEORGE, 1639-1716, Scotch, No. 104.
KELLY, REV. THOMAS, 1769-1855, No. 124.

Index to Hymns.

Songs.

State Normal School.

MORNING RESPONSES.

MONDAY.

Glo - ry be to the Fa - ther, and to the Son, and to the

Ho - ly Ghost! As it was in the be - gin-ning, is now and ev - er

shall be, world with-out end, A - men, A - men.

TUESDAY.

O praise ye the Lord, pre - pare your glad voice,

His praise in the great as-sem-bly to sing.

In their great Cre - a - tor, let Is - rael re - joice,

And chil - dren of Zi - on be glad in their King.

WEDNESDAY.

Hear our morn - ing prayer, O God! Hear our

prayer and in - cline Thine ear! A - men.

THURSDAY.

Praise the Lord, O my soul, And all that is within me,

praise His ho - ly name! Praise the Lord, O my soul,

And for - get not all His benefits! A - men.

FRIDAY.

Still, Lord, with Thee, when purple morn - ing break - eth,

When the bird waketh, and the shad - ows flee;

Fairer than morning, lovlier than the day - light,

Dawns the sweet con - scious - ness. I am with thee!

LORD'S PRAYER.

Our Father who art in heaven, Hallowed be thy name;
Give us this day our dai - ly bread;
And lead us not into temptation, but deliver us from evil:

Thy kingdom come; Thy will be done on earth as it is in heaven.
And forgive us our trespasses, as we forgive those who tres pass against us.
For thine is the kingdom, and the pow'r, and the glory for ever and ever.

A - - men.

www.ingramcontent.com/pod-product-compliance
Lightning Source LLC
Chambersburg PA
CBHW031438280326
41927CB00038B/670